The Girl Behind the Smile

♥

Dedicated to my Uncle Kenny, who lost his battle with depression, and anyone else who struggles or has struggled with mental health disorders.

I

"Stop!" I shouted at the mirror. *You're really fucking ugly. Why are you here? Remind me. Give me a reason why you should even be breathing.* I felt hot tears sting my eyes. I watched the water race down my face. I shut my eyes and ran my fingers through my hair. I paced back and forth across my room. I could smell the ham cooking out in the kitchen. I heard laughter from my brother playing his video games and the slow motion music from my sister making her videos. My phone buzzed. For a moment, I was almost distracted, but the thoughts burst into my mind again. I felt dizzy. I did a bellyflop onto my bed and threw my face into my pillow. I wanted to disappear. I wanted all of the pain built up inside of me to go away. I wanted to be dead. The girl with the perfect life. The girl behind the smile.

II

The essay

"School. Just from stating the simple noun, thousands of different emotions, memories, and experiences flood throughout your mind. To some, school is their happy place. To others, school is an everlasting inferno. School shapes us; it affects our entire future. Why should it be a such a morbid place to many people, if it's so important? Now, everyone has days he or she wishes they could just run away and never come back. I get it. I had those days for months on end. I don't want anyone else to be in that situation. We as students have been taught that bullying is wrong since before Pre-K. But when it comes down to it, do schools handle it properly? I want schools to make sure that they do everything in their power to make sure that students are as happy as the school can make them. I argue that we need a better system. There's something we aren't doing right when handling things like bullying, mental health, and eating disorders.

I'll admit, there was a time when school was my favorite place in the world. I didn't have to give myself a reason why I needed to go, or force myself to believe that today would be different from all the rest. No. I used to try in school. Even getting a B was unacceptable. School was my happy place. I felt good about myself. There wasn't a way, shape, or form that I thought very grim about myself. By that

I don't mean that I thought that I was better than everyone else, I just believed in myself. I hardly ever found myself saying that I couldn't do something. I can, I will, and I did. Back then, if you had told me that at the beginning of seventh grade my life would completely turn around, I probably would have laughed in your face. I, in fact, was living in some fantasy world. I had this notion that everything would be perfect forever. I was in my own little bubble, and nothing could affect me from the outside. Up until the first day of Jr. High, of course. I didn't know what to expect coming out of elementary school. I was only 12 and was super scared. I remember having such a fear going on inside of me while everyone seemed to be perfectly calm. They would give me a funny look when I asked questions. I was just so curious. They thought that I was crazy, but I honestly had no idea what to expect. When school came around, I was completely overwhelmed. I wasn't prepared to for the amount of homework, the difference in rules; everything caught me off guard.

I was a teenage girl who wanted to be popular. My schoolwork wasn't my number one priority, and it caused me to drastically fall behind. In my mind, being friends with everyone was what I needed to do. That's just what I did. I was the life of the party. Growing up, I had no problem making friends. As a matter of fact, I had about three people whom I considered best friends. At the time, I thought that we were unstoppable. A few fights here and there but nothing too terrible. Back then, I didn't realize how ungrateful I was. Before me, I had three amazing friends. I assumed that's how it was for everyone. That everyone had friends to drown their sorrows and wipe their tears. I made the stupid move of actually believing that everyone had someone's shoulder to cry on. I didn't notice how good I had it. I was in my own world, I never really had something big happen to me. I grew up watching everything go right in Disney movies. I always saw the problems being solved. I was never taught differently. Around sixth grade, I narrowed my best friends down to one person. No, that doesn't mean I wasn't friends with the other girls, because I was. I just had one close friend that I shared and trusted everything with. She always kept my secrets, and I kept hers. We were always having an amazing time together. She was the best friend I ever had. I loved our friendship, we rarely fought or argued. Looking back now, I see that I didn't treat her with as much respect as she deserved. She was my best friend. I should have always been there for her during tough times. She should have always been there for me too. But, it really isn't like the movies. With the other girls, it's how we treated each other. It was normal. I'm not sure, there was just something about my best friend that was different. She was more real than the rest of us. She kept secrets and didn't start drama. We continued to be best friends. Then in October of 2014, I started dating this guy named Jordan. It was a pretty decent relationship. He treated me like a princess and made my seventh-grade self really happy. But, although he was a great boyfriend, something wasn't right with our relationship. After awhile, I started to catch feelings for someone else. In my 12-year-old mind, the most logical thing to do in a situation like this would be to break up. I mean, why stay in a relationship if you're unhappy? But no. The guy was completely rude afterwards. There were times that we got along, but he did little things to bring me down. Maybe he didn't even realize he was doing it. A couple of weeks later, the guy that I liked asked me out. So being that I liked him and I was single, I said yes. So now I guess I'm a slut. A rumor started in my school that I am the biggest slut ever. Alright, let's see. The guy that I was dating, I was basically dating on and off since first grade. My relationship with Jordan was nothing serious at all. I had two relationships equal to a third-grade relationship. We only talked and the closest thing to being sexual was that we hugged. I don't understand it at all. I mean, THIS WAS SEVENTH GRADE. WHY DOES IT MATTER SO MUCH? When I asked them, 'Do you even know what a slut is?' 'Well, you move from boy to boy.' Even that, that's not a slut. I never kissed a boy. I guess breaking up with the most popular boy in the grade has consequences. Some really stupid and immature consequences, if I may add.

This continued. I felt lost. My friends were leaving me. Well, maybe they weren't. I mean, this situation wasn't a biggie. Just the occasional time that someone would forget about me. It continued throughout late January, building up to something easier to pick out.

The boys then made a pact not to date me because I'm such a 'slut.' How could someone who has had two relationships equal to a third-grade relationship be a slut? We talked, hugged, yes. 'Oh, you move from boy to boy.' Even that, how does that give you the right to give me that label? It didn't match up. My best friends label me this. After late February, times got harder. My friends were giving up on me. You could just see my self-confidence dropping lower and lower by the day. Usually, I would just go and ask my friends for advice, but they were the ones I needed advice about. March was the absolute worst month. My friends not only ignored me and excluded me, but they also started being more verbal and physical. The slut thing was their biggest comeback. After having enough and talking to my mom about it, she told me what every person said to me. 'Ignore them they're just jealous of you,' or something like that. I did not want to hear that. I went from being an energetic person to a totally dull person. That was not an easy transition for me. My best friends turning on me completely was so hard. I needed people. I needed someone at that point in my life. Of course I had my mom: she did everything she could to make me happy.

Things got worse; these events became more frequent. To top it off, some of the guys started to say I was overreacting or making this all up. But they didn't have the right to tell me this. My entire life changed just like that. I had so much stress from my schoolwork, I had to balance sports, and I had people on social media trying to start drama with me, all at once. Usually, I could deal with internet trolls, but on top of everything else going on, it became overwhelming. I could easily handle it separately. It's everyday stuff for me. I know people are mean. But all together, I was helpless. Totally vulnerable thus making me an easy target for my peers.

How was I showing my feelings? Little slits in my skin. Now, I was the type of person to think that cutting was stupid. I figured it was for attention. How is it productive by any means? I was disappointed in myself when thoughts of harming myself in any way flooded my head. I pushed and pushed and pushed them away. I don't need even more negativity in a situation like this. But my feelings controlled me. I didn't know what I was doing at first. I didn't know where to start. I looked down at my clean slate. Hmm. Just like that, I started. I felt relief, for the first time in months. A blanket of ease swept over me. How could I possibly stop? It didn't take long to realize how dumb of a decision this had been. Blood ran down my leg, and I began to cry. How did it come to this? The girl who thought life was perfect. Do I deserve this? When will I know when to give up? Locking myself in the bathroom every night and drawing with silver became a routine. I started to think about where I stood with my opinion of cutting. It's not dumb. It makes me feel good. It controls my pain. I don't do it for attention if I don't tell anyone. I cover it up every day with makeup and long clothing. Was my entire perspective on this wrong?

A couple of weeks later, someone noticed. I sat in a group with Jordan in math and he said much louder than I wanted him to, 'What happened to your arm?' I was embarrassed. The way he said it, made me feel so much worse. He sounded disgusted. I wanted to leave. Rumors spread. My phone gets one text that says "cut deeper," but unlike most, I didn't follow their instructions. It woke me up a bit. It's just fuel to their fire. Why give them what they want? At the end of March, I was cut free. That decision was one of the greatest decisions of my life. It's not worth it. Trust me.

You don't understand the pain unless you're in the situation yourself. Some people would hear my story and tell me I'm overreacting. That's fine. Losing the people who fill your life with joy, and happiness; gone. Just like that. Just, I couldn't handle being alone. People claimed they were there for me, but they never were when I needed them. I couldn't put a pin on what my grasp on this situation was. My emotion. Sad was not even close to a strong enough word. Lost: It was true, but wasn't what I was looking for. It was like an itch you can't reach. Everything's changed. My entire attitude towards everyone and everything; different. I didn't like it. No one did. I wasn't the type of person you wanted to go out for pizza with. Not anymore anyways. Plus, I am a pretty cool pizza lover.

The part that flusters me the most is my best friend; I could tell she felt bad. I could tell she wanted to talk to me. She still completely ignored me when I tried to talk to her. I was an embarrassment. She didn't want to be mean or lose our friendship, but she was under the influence of all her other friends. That loss of friendship was one of the worst feelings I have ever felt. She was my best friend. The one I could count on, the one who is always supposed to be there for me and I'm always supposed to be there for her. Just losing her was bad enough. But to lose everyone else, that was over the top. I disconnected from everything. These events continued, and they became part of life. Negativity took over me. I was completely drained of happiness. My answer to everything was 'I don't care' because honestly, I didn't care. Being too fearful, I didn't think I could ever go through with suicide. That doesn't mean I didn't think about dying because believe me, I did. Leaving behind my loving family would be too difficult. On the other hand, I wouldn't really care if I suddenly got hit by a car and died. That was my outlook on life for those couple of months; I'm not even joking. That's the disappointing part.

On the bright side, my parents finally knew that there was something seriously wrong with me. I went to the doctor. They told me that I have depression. At that point, I didn't how big of a deal it was. I just thought it was an emotion, not an actual disorder. It explains my loss of interest in everything. Nothing mattered to me. I was there, but I wasn't. Sitting in class with a blank stare, thinking about how worthless I was. It was everyday stuff for me. Going home away from people you think would be better, but they followed me. Most of the arguments were via text. On the bright side, once everybody saw how messed up I was, they stopped with the insults and even acknowledging me. They didn't want it to come to this. None of us did. We all just wanted everything to

20

be over. Everybody says there's light at the end of the tunnel. I would give a polite nod and smile while screaming skepticism throughout my head. I was so, so, sick of hearing that. When? Tell me when. I didn't know how much longer I could stand it. It changed my life. It changes how many friends you have. You push people away even though you don't mean to. You lose so much that you love. Finally, my mom had enough. She couldn't stand seeing me so different. Neither could I.

April 7th, 2015; I was free. Free from the shadows. My light at the end of the tunnel. I have remembered that day since. It was my new start, my happiness. It was well, a new school. When I started at Siren, I immediately met my new best friend, Sage Ortez. Sage is beautiful inside and out. She reminded me what it's like to have real friends. Sage showed me how friends are supposed to treat each other. We clicked right away and she guided me through my quarter of being at that school. She pulled me out of the dark place that I was in. We were always laughing at everything and having an amazing time. I had a best friend. That's what I needed.

I'm not directing this to a certain audience. Everyone deserves to know what should be done to make everyone feel safe. Everyone deserves to know that you have no idea what could be going on in someone's life. To see how others stand with our school handling certain issues, I recently sent out a survey to high school students at my school. First question, 66 of the 100 students said that they had been bullied. Next, 88.8% of students say that they see people getting bullied; 14% of which said that it was a serious, 24/7 thing. Thirdly, I asked if students felt safe at school. There was a variety of answers. Most of them said yes, but there was more than a handful that said no. Their reason? That schools don't give the right solution to bullying. So many kids, even here in this small town, don't want to go to school because of bullies. Here's the part that really needs to be heard. 'Do you believe that the school does everything in its power to make us as students happy?' Almost everybody said no. Although, it would be hard to please every student, and it's not necessarily the school's job to make students happy, still. I asked them to explain so I got better feedback. So much of what I heard was pointing out how many students go to the staff for help, or they see kids getting bullied and don't blink an eye. Is this really a school we want to represent? Where students don't feel safe at school, where students feel that school is the bad guy? It doesn't have to be.

Teachers, I know many of you would be willing to talk to a kid with their problem in a heartbeat. The students just don't know that. Put yourself out there, that you are there, that you care, you are willing to listen to whatever they need and make a difference in their life. If a student comes to you, it takes a lot of courage. Please, don't take it lightly. Listen to what they have to say. They will be so grateful. If someone is truly hurting, they appreciate it when someone is there for them beyond words. You will be their hero. Some teachers feel that they don't have time to get to know a student well enough for some one-on-one talking. Well, how about having weekly or even monthly, quick, classroom meetings? Talk to them as a whole. Some kids may want to keep their feelings private. I suggest putting out a box - anything kept private only for your eyes - where students can put in anything at any time without having their peers know about it, if that's what they'd prefer. Together, we can stop this. Together, we can make a difference.

If I had known my options of being able to talk to teachers and other adults, my life would be completely different right now. If we had a better, more public system for kids who are depressed, suicidal, lost, or simply just need someone to talk to, you'd gain respect for so many students. If it were different last year, I wouldn't have lost all of my confidence. I could be myself without constantly worrying, I could raise my hand in class without having an anxiety attack, I could talk to someone without thinking of every single flaw I have. I could go to bed without deep down wishing I wouldn't wake up. I could wake up without having this burning feeling that I'm not supposed to be here. This is what depression does to a person. I found the help and happiness I need right now. I'm the happiest I've been in a long time. This is me. Why not share the information with others to stop all of this madness. We need to lay down the law for kids who think it's okay to bully. We need to make sure that kids aren't going to continue to kill themselves because they believe that that's the only route to happiness and ease again. Is 4,400 a big number to you when it comes to death? That's how many children commit suicide a year. Not to mention that 14% of high school students have seriously thought about suicide and half of those young adults have tried. Do you want to make a difference? Take a stand and start here."

III

Introduction

Hi, I'm Camryn Nasman. I am 14 years old. What you've read so far is what I started with. I had an assignment to write an argumentative essay, and that was over a year ago. All of that with getting depression, and losing my friends, that was over two years ago now. I remember everyone was arguing about if people should be able to drive sooner, or schools start later, but I wanted to choose a topic that would make a difference locally. In seventh grade, I developed depression. It flipped my entire world around and the way that schools handled it drove me completely insane. After a while, I kept finding myself going back to this piece of writing. I was extremely proud of myself. (I got an A by the way.) Since then, I've been writing. In this book, you will read about my daily battle with depression, anxiety and suicidal thoughts. You will read about my struggle with self-harm. You will read my story. This is The Girl Behind the Smile.

IV

One year later

I finally remembered how it felt to be happy. I can't begin to put into words the amount of happiness that surged through my body. The girl who wanted nothing more than to be dead; happy. How could I ever let that go? You're probably reading this thinking I'm nuts. I don't care. It was the first time since being at this school in my eighth grade year that I felt like I belonged. I felt like I could accomplish things in life. I could tell jokes and be myself again without having to worry about people judging me for just being myself. I've never felt anything better than this. What in the world could bring such a depressed girl back to the top? Friends. I had friends who finally showed me how friends are supposed to treat each other. We got along so well. We went together like peas and carrots, as we would say. The best part is, it was with people I would have never even thought about talking to. And there I was, happy. I wanted to cry, but for the right reason this time.

V

Imagine, you're looking for the perfect wedding dress. You look high and low for the special gown, and you just can't seem to find the right one. Of course, you have many other wedding dresses all around you; people keep saying, "You look great in all of them, just pick one." But you as the bride know that you must have the perfect gown. You unexpectedly run into an unknown dress shop on your way to lunch. And there you see it. It's almost like you can hear it calling your name. It's everything you've ever imagined. Running the fastest you've ever seen yourself run, you try on the dress. You're in love all over again. You take out your wallet: you have just enough money. Excited, you go to pay for the dress.

"Excuse me, ma'am, no niggers allowed." Says a snarky worker.

"Um, no, excuse me." You politely respond.

"You heard me; I don't need my customers in the presence of you. Leave before I call the police."

"Maybe there's a rational conclusion that we could come to. I have the money; I could buy the dress and never come back."

"Hmm, no. Someone who is deserving will stumble upon it."

You walk away knowing that there's nothing you can do. It's out of your control. The pain eats you alive. Just like that, your dreams are crushed. Making matters even more stressful, it's something that you have zero control over.

It obviously wasn't this extreme for me, but it sure felt like it during that time. I was so happy, right? Then I get my happiness stolen from me for a totally wrong reason. Now, my friends are high schoolers, and I'm an eighth grader. Big whoop. They are told that they can't talk to me, or else they will get suspended, just because I'm in middle school. I could see the principal putting restrictions on our friendship if we were to be making out in the halls or some stupid shit like that. Yeah, that's definitely a situation to act upon. But this, this was over the top for me. I finally find happiness. Do you know how difficult that is? Every day for a year, I told myself, "There's light at the end of the tunnel. Things will get better." Every single day was a battle for me. So many days I just wanted to end everything and be done. But because of my encouraging words to myself, I held on. The day that I met John, I knew what I meant by saying things were going to get better. Let me tell you, John and I didn't have that weird moment when you first meet. It was never awkward between us. As soon as we first started talking, it was like I knew him my entire life. It was simply like we started up an unfinished conversation from the day before. I never met anyone in my life, other than him, where I had that. I knew right away that he would make a huge impact on my life. We were never "dating." We understood that we couldn't. I didn't have approval from my parents, and he respected that. John made me feel beautiful. I loved the person that I was when I was around him. I wasn't with him because he made me feel like I had worth, I loved the person that he was. Feeling worth something felt amazing too, though. It felt so awesome to remember how it felt to have a purpose. John showed me my future. With depression, you cannot see the future. It's like a block in the road. He removed the wall. My future, it was clear. Never, ever, ever, has anyone else had that effect on me. It felt amazing. Everything seemed so close in time, and I felt I had the power to accomplish them. I was living again. Everything was going better than it had

in a long time. It felt too good to be
true. I liked John a lot. We knew that
we couldn't be together. So, we
weren't. But we did share our dreams,
passions, similar interests -
everything.

VI

One night I'm sitting at home being lazy, as usual. Suddenly, two of John's friends text me and say, "John's cheating on you." Now, hard to cheat on someone when you aren't dating, right? But you see, I liked John, and he liked me. We weren't in a committed relationship, but I thought of him as more than a friend, as he did to me. That night I found out he had been receiving nudes from other girls - or so people were telling me. People sent me pictures of him kissing another girl. I couldn't handle it. It broke me, and I'm good with handling breakups and whatnot. I cried and cried and cried. I completely opened up to John. I trusted him; I shared with him things I have never told another living soul.

How did I react to it? I threw my body onto my bed and let the tears temporarily stain my pillow. I was taken advantage of by one of the few people who could light up my world. Suddenly, I had an urge. The urge to do something I haven't done in over a year. I locked my bedroom door and grabbed one of my two sharp blades. Last year, when I first started to cut, I was new to it. When you first start off cutting, they aren't going to be deep. But with time, those little scratches form into massive hacks in your skin that never seem to fade. At that point, I wasn't as knowledgeable on the subject. I started cutting last year thinking that it would build up my courage to kill myself someday; that hurting myself on purpose will make it easier in the long run when it was time. I never used it as a stress reliever. In the moment a couple of weeks ago, I couldn't handle it. I had to escape. I was hitting things, throwing things, screaming into a pillow. Finally, I lay there seeming almost lifeless, and cried until I didn't think that I could anymore. Just when I thought that I was over it, I turn on my phone. I see a picture of John and I as the background. The anger rose inside of me, and I couldn't take it anymore. I grabbed my pocket knife and spread the skin apart all across my left arm. I kept going. This pleased me. It relaxed me. It seemed to take all the weight off of me. How bad did I cut? Well, it was my first time in a year since I did it, so the cuts weren't very deep at all. How many were there? A lot. There was barely a visible place left. But most of them were not deep. Just scratches. It made me feel something that nothing else could fill. I wanted to die. I wanted to go under a rock and never come out. Suddenly, I heard a car pull in. Whom could it be at this time of night?

VII

My Knights in Shining Armor

My friends Luke and Noah came over, out of nowhere, because they knew that I was upset. I was very grateful to have friends by my side at this point. We had a great time hanging out. Once you go through a traumatic situation, you learn a lot. I learned to be thankful for more things in life. Not everybody has a best friend. I'm not oblivious to when people try to be here for me. I don't brush it off anymore as something people are obligated to do. It's a choice. I appreciate it when people try to help. That's what my friends did. They helped me. Made me laugh. They distracted me. Now I'm going to go out of context here for a moment to tell you what I exactly mean by "distracting me." The life that I live every day, I am always upset. Every moment that I am alone, in my thoughts; I am unhappy. But there are certain things, certain people in my life that can distract me for a period of time. I can say I am happy. It usually doesn't last too long, but I remember what it feels like to be alive. So, when I say "distracting" I mean I forget about everything and push it away for a while. Once I find distractions, I tend to hold them very close to me. Letting them go would be stupid. My friend Luke saw my arm and looked up at me in shock. I was panicking inside my head. I didn't know what to say. Luke noticed my embarrassment and said, "That's badass." I felt relieved. Luke's liked me for a while now. He's a Junior, and I'm an Eighth-grader. It would be weird for us to date. He is super cute, though.

VIII

Life with suicidal thoughts isn't really what people think it is. There're many people in this school, in my grade, who believe that faking depression is something that makes you cooler. It's a living hell. Not going to sugar coat it. Having suicidal thoughts isn't the same as having depression, but it is something that may come with it. It's not the simple "something-bad-happened- I-want-to-die" type deal. No, having suicidal thoughts doesn't mean now and then wondering what would happen if you killed yourself. It's not wondering how your life being taken would affect the lives of your friends, family, and other peers. It's not having a bad day and thinking to yourself, "I should kill myself, I wish that I was dead." No. It's sitting in the middle of class and hearing a voice more powerful than your own telling you that you don't belong here; you're worthless. It's laughing at some funny memes late at night and feeling a liquid substance of negativity roll down your throat. It's a barrel of all the reasons you shouldn't be given life, thrown at you. It's without any warning at all. It seems as if it's not even yourself speaking. It's something else taking you over and pointing out all the wrong you've done. That's what having suicidal thoughts means. Nothing angers me more than people who think "I should go tell all of my friends that I have depression, so they feel bad for me." I understand that everyone has a battle of his or her own, that everyone has secrets, and thoughts, and actions that people don't know about. I get it. But there's a big difference in a bad life and a bad day. Every day, every single day of my life, I think about killing myself. It's not a choice. I'm learning to cope with it. I'm learning to ignore the thoughts and how to deal with them. Yes, it's difficult, but I constantly find myself saying, "Camryn Nasman, you have worth, you have potential. Things will get better. I know you get sick of hearing it. It might be today, tomorrow, next month or three years from now, but you will find the meaning of everything once again. Something will show up in your life proving your words right." Sometimes, it gets really difficult to believe myself. I get so negative and I push the positive words away. Something that keeps me going is

thinking about all the people I help
and all the advice I give. I love
helping people and want to do it more.
It makes me feel good when I do. It
hurts me to see people upset.

IX

Something that I cannot seem to wrap my mind around, is why anyone would want to pretend that they have depression. Honestly, it's not something people should WANT to have. If someone wants attention that bad, I don't know what to tell them. I don't understand. I don't at all. There are people like me who have depression and want nothing more than to be better. We want to be cured and be able to wake up every morning without trying to convince ourselves that there's a purpose. It will come naturally, like it used to. We want our lives back. But at the same time, some people want nothing more than to have depression. They crave the attention. People like that are completely clueless to the topic. They obviously don't understand what a burden it is to have. It's not something that you can just ignore; it's always there, and it's always dragging you down. People can think that it's okay, but it's not. Depression is a trend. I seriously do not understand why people think it's okay to fake depression. It's like faking autism. Why would you fake a disorder? It's the same concept. What good would it do to fake it? Some people may just simply believe that they have depression. Maybe they don't understand that it's not just a rough patch in the road. It's more than being sad. It's a genuine, serious health concern.

X

Back to having my new friends, I am very grateful for them. They show me how friends are supposed to treat each other. That's not something to brush off. I wish that I could go back in time to the beginning of seventh grade. I would open my eyes and appreciate what I had before me. Not only great friends, but confidence. Before I could wear the ugliest outfits and not even think of it. I'd have a face full of blemishes and not think any differently about myself. But now, I have to look at myself in the mirror a million times to see if I look acceptable. If I even have one pimple, I feel like that's what all attention is going to; nothing else. I wish I could go back to the old me. The one who thought they were worth a lot, thought they had a future, and there wasn't a doubt about it in their mind. I want to be there again. Part of me is fine with the way I am. I'm not going to go run to everyone and be like, "I'm so fat and ugly." There's a difference between low self-esteem and fishing for compliments. The part that I'm happy about is that I don't look past the fact that people try to help me. I notice when people try to help me in any way. I can't stress enough how much I took for granted, and how stupid I feel. I didn't know any better. It never came to my mind that there's a lot of people who don't have the support system that I did. But now I know. Going through that situation did show me a lot. I feel a lot wiser from going through it, even though it caused a lot of pain. In the long run, it probably helped me more than it hurt me. Maybe it was for the best. The pain of going through that situation is temporary while appreciating people, and not taking people for granted, will last a lifetime.

XI

So where am I now? Good question.
I'm getting help. I've stopped cutting
again. On a Saturday night I had the
urge to cut. All day I was distracted
by volleyball, of course. My mom and I
talked about what's going on in my
life, and for the first time this
school year, I felt like we were on the
same page again. I used to be able to
talk with my mom about everything under
the sun. Now I am afraid to talk to her
for the same reason I don't talk to
other people; lack of understanding.
Life hasn't been the easiest for my mom
these past couple months either. I
don't know how she manages to get
everything done without having a mental
breakdown every hour. She does an
outstanding job of being my mother. I

wouldn't trade her for anything. Lately, I've seen us drifting apart. My seeking advice usually ends in yelling and misunderstanding. Slowly we haven't been able to talk about anything personal at all. She never agrees with anything I have to say. So, I've been doing my thing. Trying to figure things out on my own. When I reached my limit, I would cut, and that was what replaced my mom's helpful words. It soothed my frustration. But, Saturday my mom and I went and bought a sketching notebook and different colored pencils as an alternative to cutting. I had fun with her. When I got home, A LOT of drama was being thrown at me. I wanted to cut so, so, so, bad. I fought the urge. After drawing for a solid two hours, I asked Luke if he would FaceTime me, so I wouldn't do something stupid. Being the awesome person that he is, he called me. We talked for 13 hours straight. I wasn't even thinking about cutting. I knew as soon as we would stop talking I would start thinking negatively again and try to cut. So, Luke stayed on FaceTime with me from 9 pm from 10 am talking about life. I used to have a big crush on Luke, so it felt pretty good to talk. We just talked about life and told stories. I was never distant from Luke when I had a crush on John. We just didn't talk as much as we normally would when I started liking John. Then it hit me. How much he does for me. He drives over when I'm upset, brings me food, checks in on me, is there when I need someone to talk to, no matter what. He stays up late to make sure I won't do something I'll regret. Luke has been there since day one; he actually wants to listen to what I have to say. He absorbs what I have to say. This guy, he checks in on me all the time. I couldn't ask for a better friend. My mom likes Luke, too. Luke knows how much I dislike school. I've told him my story. He wants to look out for me; he doesn't want to see me in the state that I was in last year. So, Luke talks to me every chance he can; he wants to make sure I was all good. I appreciate it so much. I appreciate it from anybody and everybody who helps me through this.

XII

You see the personal me. The one people don't know. Now, what do my peers at school see? I'm a very popular girl. I love making people laugh more than anything. I bounce from group to group; I don't belong to a particular group of people. I'm friends with basically everybody. To them, I'm the dumb girl who likes to make a lot of jokes. I'm the girl who challenges her guy friends to farting contests. To them, I'm very confident and kind of go with the flow. The laid-back girl who has a lot of respect towards others and always gets doubles on lunch and out eats all the guys at the lunch table. I'm not faking anything. It's me. It's the part of me that I choose to put on display. However, with every funny joke, I have my anxiety freaking out saying, "What if they don't laugh? What if they think I'm trying too hard or annoying or weird?" With every mean comment that I hear, I have my depression telling me that it's true. With every homework assignment, I have the anxiety telling me that I need to do this if I want to have an awesome future. I can't have my teachers think lowly of me. I must succeed. Then there's the depression that tells me that I can't do anything. It completely drains all of the motivation out of my body. People think that telling me the importance of getting good grades will affect any of my decisions whether or not I am going to try my hardest in school. With depression, you cannot see the future. You don't see yourself graduating high school or buying your first home; it's the present and the past. So, trying to explain how critical getting good grades is for someone with depression, won't get you very far. It's like a wall blocking off your future. This is also me. There are just certain parts of me that I want people to see. That's where the label "dumb" comes into play. I don't get the best of grades so therefore I am dumb. But honestly, I want nothing more than to be an excellent student. I want to turn in homework and make my parents proud. This isn't something that I can explain to my teachers, and even if I did, they probably wouldn't understand. It's not my choice whether I'm with it or not. Sometimes it just takes me over. My mom always pushed me to do my best in school, but she didn't understand at that point in time how messed up I was. This is really hard to explain. I don't have the drive to do anything. Try to imagine it's like the devil/angel thing. Only one is the devil, and the other one is the devil's cousin. There isn't a good guy in this. One's freaking out, almost hyper speed, shouting all that could go wrong and why you should be worried. It's constantly making you double-check. You can't even order at McDonald's without freaking out. It takes a lot of your confidence away. You depend on a lot of people. Being alone, and doing things alone, scares you. You don't want to be embarrassed in front of people. That's what mine is. Everyone has had some form of anxiety arise inside them. It can be jitters before a big speech or butterflies when your crush gives you a hug. Everyone has had some minor

anxiety. But that's still not the same
as having an anxiety disorder. I mean,
that's just the mental part of it. The
physical part of it makes you sweat a
lot. It makes you shake. Say goodbye to
sleep, too. You can't even eat or drink
in front of someone without worrying.
The other devil acts as a vacuum and
takes away all of your drive,
motivation and replaces it with a lack
of interest in things that usually make
you happy. You disconnect from everyone
and everything with no questions asked.
Again, it's not your choice. You can't
just wake up and say I want to be a
straight A student. You can't say, I
want to be the best I can today. That's
hardly possible without help. You see
no future. Nothing is enjoyable. Sure,
there are times you can feel great, you
can even be happy. But it doesn't last

long. It's just something always there seemingly holding you back from greatness. It's having no answers for the problems you face. Every single morning you feel the weight of your worthlessness in your chest. I could go on and explain to you what these devils do to the people who are affected by them every single day of their lives, but it's not the same imagining it as it is living it.

XIII

On April 20, I was extremely depressed: more than usual. I had 0% motivation and was drained. The day was going by very, very slowly. I wasn't talking much, and I almost fell asleep in 2nd and 3rd hour. By the time choir came around, I had thought that I was going to pass out. I couldn't even keep my eyes open to sing. For about a week, people had been asking me what the big scars on my arms were. I always jokingly said I was attacked by a bear, then we'd share a laugh and move on. That Wednesday was not like the others. I felt like I held the weight of the world on my shoulders. One of my seventh-grade friends kept asking what was on my arm and I'd say the same thing as I did before. This time we did not laugh. Over and over again he asked me what was on my arm. A couple of other students joined in pestering me to tell them. I could feel myself getting angry and upset. My old friend kept telling everyone to stop, but they didn't obey. Finally, one kid yelled, "She cuts herself." It got quiet. Then the kids flooded me with questions to ask if it was true. I snapped. I got up and walked right out of the classroom. Now, the kid must not have known any better but you never, ever, point out somebody's scars. To you, it's just scar tissue on somebody's arm, but to them, it's a reminder of the pain and suffering that they've gone through. There are two different types of people when it comes to cutting. Those who use cutting as an outlet; it temporarily stops their pain. And those who cut for attention. The difference between the two is the people who use the cutting as an outlet cannot let people see their cuts. The people who cut for attention will show them off to people. They will tell everyone and have no shame behind each slit. But let me tell you something, that Wednesday was one of the first days that I told myself to be confident in a short sleeve shirt. I was cut free for over a month at that point. They were no longer cuts, as they were scars. Why should I be so embarrassed? It's not like they were fresh, it doesn't make me a bad person. The reason that I stormed out of that room was that with each scar on my arm, there's a story. I remember how each one of those got there. I remember the night, the reason, everything. It takes me back to a point in my life that I'm trying to let go. No, I am not proud of my cuts. I don't want to show them off to the world; I don't want to post a picture of them on Facebook. I just want to be comfortable again. The courage of wearing a short sleeve shirt or a tank top after you quit cutting must be very, very high. You can't just wake up and say, "Yup, I'm going to wear a short sleeve shirt today because I feel like it." It's just not possible. So there I was, a day I had courage and felt like it was safe to show my arms once again, they were pointed out. I was so ashamed of myself. I kept thinking so negatively. My self-confidence dropped. Why couldn't I be like normal kids, why do I have to be such a screw up? I wanted my life back, I wanted everything to be different. I went home, and really

thought about drawing art on my skin
once again, but remembered why I was
angry in the first place.

XIV

March 17th was the last day that I cut. On March 18th, I woke up with the same old feeling that I didn't belong, only stronger. I felt like I was dead. I had this notion that I wasn't even living, it was super weird. I woke up that Friday at 7:00 which is the time that the bus comes. My mom had to do some work around the house, so I got dressed and waited around for her. It didn't feel real; I felt like I was in a dream. It's really hard to explain. Everything gets blurry, and I feel like I'm not there. Certain times in my life I catch myself wondering if I'm still alive, or still riding four-wheeler, or still on the boat. I feel so detached from everything around me that I have the need to ask myself if I'm really even in my body anymore. When I was younger, I would describe myself as feeling like a zombie. This has happened a lot and recently found out that it's something called depersonalization. This opened up a whole new world to me. Researching this, I discovered that It's caused when I'm lost in my thoughts - which does happen very often, especially at this point in my life - but it's a result of depression and or anxiety, which I happen to have both. Moving back to this treacherous day, I had that feeling when I woke up. I took it as a sign of death. In my entire life, I never thought about dying so much. I never had such want to die. The previous month before that, I'd been really sick, so I complained to my mom about it. "There's ibuprofen on the counter." At that moment, I had such an uneasy, yet satisfying feeling. Death. Everybody has their personal belief on what dying would be like. Mine is kind of like, if it's my time, it's my time. Never had I ever been so certain that it was my time. My eyes burned as I walked up to the bottle of the pills. What was I doing? I had no idea. I had no idea what kind of pills would do the trick to end my life, or how many to finish off the job. Completely clueless. I remember standing there with the same old feeling that I was in a dream, staring at the pills. At that moment, I tried to think of what all I've accomplished in life, and my favorite memories, I thought of nothing. How is this possible? I know that I've accomplished things in life, I knew I've been proud of myself and laughed a lot. But why I couldn't think of one single thing at that moment, beats me. I took that as a sign. If at the age of 14, I couldn't think of one thing I accomplished or one memory that I've had fun in, I didn't deserve to live. That was my perspective on it. So, I picked up the bottle and took two pills at first. Then another and another until I was completely drained. I didn't know what I was doing, of course. I didn't know that 200-milligram ibuprofen couldn't kill you if you took too many, but that's not what I went into the situation thinking. My intentions were to kill myself. Even though it wouldn't have worked, I didn't know that. Shortly after I took the pills, I got super sick. During the time after I took the pills, and went to school, I got the opportunity to open my eyes a bit. I sang. My mom and I sang together for the first time since I can remember. It was a major factor in my opinion on life. There I was, feeling a bit more alive. It was just a small taste of reality. Afterwards, we left for school. I trudged on through the last half of the school day as I do every single day. I felt as if I had a knot in my stomach so tight even Mary herself could not help me.

There was a dance that night. I am on student council, so I had to stay after to help decorate. After working on that for a couple of hours, I had to rush home to get ready. I didn't have any time so I threw on a dress and left. I didn't do my hair or anything. As soon as I got there, I realized my

huge mistake. My dress was sleeveless.
My body seemed to freeze in time, but
my thoughts did the opposite. Oh no. I
looked around. Alright, maybe they
won't notice. Maybe they won't look. I
walked into the room filled with the
people I've been growing up with. I've
never feared so many familiar faces in
my life. All of a sudden, people
whispered. People's eye wandered to my
arm. I was scared. I tried my best to
still have fun. I danced a little bit
but I was overthinking the entire time.
I felt a giant tug on my arm, I was
being forced somewhere. I looked up to
see my mom. She led me into the
bathroom and pointed at my arm,
demanding answers. I was embarrassed. I
was disappointed in myself. I didn't
know how to approach the situation. I
started to tear up, and walk away. She

started yelling at me and finally, let me leave. I threw on a really big, baggy sweatshirt that I had and looked like a hobo. My night was basically ruined. I stood by myself and leaned aginst the wall and watched as everybody else had fun, but me. About 30 minutes later, my mom showed up and threw a bag at me. It was leggings, and a pink long-sleeved shirt. She understood. I ran into the bathroom and changed. My night turned around a little bit.

XV

I almost made it two months without cutting. The way that I got that far was to find different outlets for all of the pain and stress. My first go-to would be to go outside and listen to music for about an hour. If I was still upset after that, I would go in the woods and break sticks and hit dead trees or something. It lets a lot of anger out. If I wanted to cut, I would also draw pictures. Not all of the pictures that I drew were positive. Heck, most of them weren't. It still got my mind off of things; I felt good. My favorite thing to do is to write, though. It empowers me more than anything. If you struggle with cutting,

I highly suggest writing or drawing.
Well, anything that you're good at, or
like doing.

XVI

Life has been really confusing for me lately. I'm learning not to dwell on the past as much. My life quotes are, "If it's meant to be, it'll be. Everything happens for a reason." It reminds me not to worry about things that aren't in my control which is what I guess a significant portion of my stress is. My family is going downhill. My parents are thinking about separating, and there are certain moments where it doesn't seem to bother me, and I reflect on how cool the opportunity would be to start over. Then late at night or whenever I'm lost in my thoughts I think about how my mom isn't financially stable. I think about how my dad won't be able to do all of the things my mom does for him. I don't know if he or she can live without each other. I'm scared. Everyone in this situation is scared.

Update My parents are going to work things out. Everything will be normal again.

It's funny. I wrote that thinking that everything was going to turn out just fine. I thought that everything would be the same. Isn't that just hilarious? My dad left. Now, what? I thought it would be a cool experience for us, but it's not as "cool" as I thought it would be. I don't show it to my mom but, this is really messing me up. My dad is gone. He wasn't just the guy who paid the bills. He was my dad. I saw him cry for the first time just a couple of weeks before my parents separated. But the night that I was so "sick" and had to leave my friend's house, I recognized my dad for the first time in years. My dad wasn't the grumpy, unhappy guy who always yelled at us. His tear-filled eyes didn't look like the bad guy; he looked truly hurt. It was odd seeing him like this. His eyes stone cold for all my teenage years so far were never welcoming. Heck, my dad doesn't even know I have depression or anxiety. My mom just recently told him that I used to cut. My dad knows the same me that I put on display to my peers at school; the funny one who doesn't care what people think. My dad doesn't know that when he tells me to go order my food at McDonald's, there's such a fear going on inside my head. My dad doesn't know that the reason I can't sleep at night is because of my ever-running thoughts speeding around in my head. Completely clueless that I'm so messed up. So the feeling I got the night I went home "sick," was very… different.

XVII

It's Sunday, May 1st. I need to make sure that I'm not dead already. I'm getting so caught up in everything. I feel like there's so much I need to accomplish, but there's also a much more powerful feeling telling me that there's nothing left for me to do. Honestly, not knowing any talents of mine, and not knowing accomplishments I've experienced, are really getting me down. The way that I try to get through things is by finding different outlets for certain emotions. Like I've mentioned before, drawing, listening to music, and writing are my getaways. I wish I could have finished this book.

The End

I decided not to pull the trigger…
Yet. First, I need to write notes to my
friends, family and everyone else I
care about.

XVIII

Several people asked me if I was alright and I'd smile and say "I'm good" because it's turned into a natural response now. I lied. I lie all the time when it comes to how I'm feeling. Well, the exact definition is "an intentionally false statement." I don't really mean to lie; I just want to keep my feelings private. My mom recently brought up a good point. We were fighting and arguing back and forth. Ending the argument, she said, "You're just a bitch that likes the attention." I just walked away. Depression is something really hard for people to understand. Even before I learned about it, I didn't think it was really anything at all. As I mentioned before, I thought that it was an emotion, not a disorder. But what my mom said, really got me thinking. Of course, shortly afterward she apologized and further explained what she meant. The impression that I got from her words was that she was telling me that I was faking this all to be an attention whore. We weren't at the same understanding, though. As she explained her thoughts, I realized what she meant. Alright, so, it's not like I don't have good days, because trust me, I do. When I'm at school, I try to surround myself with people who make me feel good about myself instead of bringing me down. This was also a big transition for me. It's much easier said than done just to get up and change friends. But I did it and I'm very glad I did. I'm not an outcast when it comes to school. I'm basically friends with everybody in my grade, I just don't have a best friend. I keep my circle small and don't tell most people anything. If I was close friends with you, you would know. When new people find out about me, they are utterly shocked. I'm a very outgoing person. When it comes to my reputation at school, people usually think of the always-hyper girl because that's how I play out every day. It's me trying to be happy, and trying to distract myself. It's starting to get much better. School days aren't totally unbearable anymore. So, when people would catch a glimpse of my scars or see me cry, it would thoroughly confuse them. How could someone like me be so "depressed" without it being fake and for attention? Let me tell you, yes, it's possible for me and anyone else like me to be happy. I try not to take my problems out on people while at school. However, it doesn't always work. When I go home, it's my time to think. That's where the negativity can overpower my positive thoughts. When I don't have things to take my mind off of all the bad stuff - which is usually when I'm alone or lost in my thoughts - I'm sad. Depression is tough for people to understand, and it's difficult for me to try to get people to understand what it really is. So just because someone seems happy and outgoing, doesn't mean that they are on the inside. "Fake it until you make it." is a quote I often hear people use. I'll say it, time and time again; everyone has fears, issues, doubts, secrets. Everyone is fighting their own battle; everyone has a story to tell. But behind these emotions are dreams, hopes, and desires. You can't let your fear take the place of your dreams.

XIX

You know when you're sitting at home watching TV and one of the characters on the show says, "What could go wrong?" or "Nothing worse could possibly happen." and then the most horrible thing that could possibly go wrong, goes wrong? Well, that's what happened to me. Reading this book, you've probably noticed that I have been getting a lot more progress when it comes to my depression, anxiety or suicidal thoughts. That's what I thought too. Everything was going to be alright. I'm not telling you this to scare you at all. It's not my intention whatsoever, but I was going to kill myself.

Plain and simple as that. Nothing more. I had a plan, I wrote letters, everything you could possibly think of to prepare for suicide, I did it. Ready as I'll ever be, I thought. But the thing is, I didn't want to die. I wanted to live. Sometimes I think people confuse wanting to die and just wanting to be found or wanting happiness again. The feelings are oh, so, close. They both make you feel like garbage. And it's about time to take out the trash.

XX

Just your average day. Nothing to tick me off in the morning. No fighting with my brother or sister. But, I did, in fact, have an argument with my mom about using a curling iron wrong and dirty track clothes. I grabbed some Cheetos and walked out the door to the bus. - Actually, scratch that. - I ran out the door with no shoes on. I was in a hurry to get to hell - er, I mean school.

Almost off the bus, I get accompanied by Luke. We walk the halls and talk for as much time as we can before having to go to class. Luke, he knows something is wrong with me. He always can put a smile on my face. Any and every time, except today. I woke up upset. Nothing new. But, this time was different. My body was completely drained of hope. Nothing, nada. Again, I caught myself asking, "Am I even alive?" No. I am not alive. I'm breathing. Existing. However, I am not living. Sometimes, I get a taste of what it's like to live. I remember that there's something more to life than just breathing. Sadly, that's not too often. I've actually been really happy lately. When Luke can't make me happy, there's something really wrong with me. So May, 9th, when he couldn't make me even lose my stare from the floor, you think that he would notice my sadness. The problem with him is, like most people, he doesn't know how to handle these types of situations. Most people don't have to go through things like this. Either if they are the ones helping, or the ones in need of help, most people wouldn't know how to react. His intentions are good; he doesn't like seeing me unhappy. That day, he didn't give me a boost of, "Hey, Camryn, you know that I care about you, right?" Or at least I didn't see it. Every ounce of hope I can get is helpful. He continued to talk. Completely oblivious to my pain. I listened patiently. He finally asked if I was okay, and I lied to him. My mind screamed at my heart not to tell him, so I didn't. I'm not sure if it was a good or bad thing, but he didn't second guess. He continued to talk about stupid shit that I couldn't care less about at the moment. It sounds like a mean thing to say, but it's true. Nothing else was on my mind other than killing myself. I can't talk to him about it no matter how badly I needed to be reminded that I was special or how bad I just needed a hug. You see, Luke never just listens to what I have to say. It always turns into his problem, which never really bothered me, up until this point. Now, I have to get to class. That day, we had to do some work out in the commons instead of keyboarding because of high school testing. There really wasn't anything in particular different about this day besides one thing. At a glance from my perspective, it would look like it would turn out to be a really good day. Boy, was I wrong. To occupy myself, I read a book. Coincidentally, It was about a girl who commits suicide. I absolutely loved it. I convinced myself to stop reading this book. But why? It empowered me. But not in the right way.

It gave me fuel to kill myself. I couldn't just walk away from it. I finished the book during first hour. I laid on the table seat in the commons. For the past two weeks, all I wanted to do was cry, but I couldn't. And right there, I wanted to cry so bad, but all I could do was stare off at something and feel my heart slowly breaking. I don't want to die. "Please give me a sign that I belong," I kept screaming in my head. But the little voice inside of me replayed all of my flaws, all of my bad choices, and all the wrong I've done. A kick in the gut it felt like. I was already dead. I didn't have any purpose here. I trudged into second period with my mind made up, I was going to kill myself.

"Can I go talk to Mrs. W?"

What in the world was I doing? Before I knew it, I was up asking my science teacher if I could leave class. I was finally crying while walking down the hall to seek help.

A substitute teacher said, "Good morning Camryn, how are you?"

"I'm good, how are you?" I said with my head down, while tears rolled down my face.

I looked in the office, the secretary that I trusted was gone that day. I walked by the guidance counselor's office; there was somebody in there. I couldn't go back to class. I was a wreck. Without hesitation, I walked down the hallway towards the Junior High classrooms. It didn't feel real when I went into my social studies teacher's classroom and asked, "Can I talk to you?" Normally, it would have taken all of the courage in my body to go ask for help, especially from a teacher. It didn't even feel like it was me. My teacher said yes and lead me out into the hallway.

"I need help."

"With what?"

"I'm going to kill myself."

We talked a little bit, but not about anything relevant to the situation at hand. I could hear the concern in her voice. She wanted to help, but I don't think that she knew how to. She did her best and asked if I wanted to go talk to the principal. With the situation with John Green, I wasn't quite fond of her. So, I

declined over dramatically like it was
the worst possible thing that could
happen. She then put me into a dark
room and disappeared. I'd like to tell
you my thought process in my time alone
in that room, but I don't remember. It
was a blur. Next thing I knew, my
guidance counselor appeared in the room
and led me into her office. We hardly
talked. I just told her my plan, and
she put me on the phone with someone
who would "help me." They didn't give
me a hand at all. My mind was made up,
why did I seek help? Well, like I said
before, I honestly and truly didn't
want to die, I just felt like it was
the only option for me to be happy
again. The part of me that wanted to
live; jumped out. You're reading this
from a girl who has many dreams. You're
reading this from a girl that wants to

live. The simple things like the sound of someone's laugh, or the taste of my favorite food, I would forget. I would be numb. No feeling whatsoever.

I was on the line with the suicide hotline. The information I had to give out wasn't to help me. Address, number, family. Not even a, "Please don't kill yourself." That's all I wanted to hear at that point. Even though I thought my mind was made up, maybe it wasn't. I just wanted to hear someone tell me no. I needed a sign not to die, and I didn't get it.

Phone calls were made to my parents, and I was left alone again. I got a sign. Sometimes we get so caught up in waiting for a sign when in reality, getting no sign is also a sign. If people really cared, why would they leave someone ready to die alone? No one asked me if I was alright or how I was feeling at the moment. It was perfectly clear that people wanted to help and tried their best, but in my mind, I was alone. Nobody could say or do the right thing. I'm going to kill myself, I kept repeating in my head. I spun around it the chair as fast as I could and screamed, "I'm going to die" over and over again in my head. Then my mom shows up.

Now, I'm at the local hospital peeing in cups and getting blood drawn left and right. My Grandma left work to come see me. Several doctors and nurses check in with me. This process lasted three hours. I've recently started to hate going to the doctor, only because of my cuts. At that point, it didn't even matter anymore. They knew why I was there. After what seemed to be years were over with, my mom, grandma and I set off to Eau Claire. I was being admitted to the hospital; a bigger hospital. I had no idea what to expect. I read the rules and regulations in several big packets that the other hospital gave me. It sounded like a prison. How bad can it be? I tried to have a positive mind about it. "I'm getting help. It's what I want… what I need." It was helpful up to the point of walking into the big hospital. It was the most traumatic event I have ever experienced, hands down. It didn't feel real. We were escorted by a guard through a long hallway until we got to a set of elevators. My mother and I were crying. I couldn't go. I was so, so scared. After waiting, we saunter onto the elevator getting closer and closer to my misery stay. We went up a couple of floors and had to leave all of our stuff in a locker. Everything. My mom couldn't have her phone, lanyard; nothing. We then followed the man through two sets of locked doors. There it was. The point of no return. As I mentioned before, I haven't been able to cry over anything for a month or two. But there I was: crying. The tears ran down my face as if all the beauty in the world had vanished before my eyes. Nurses greeted me at the door; patients looked at me funny. I tried to take in my surroundings quickly. "I don't want to stay here." I said to my mom. We were both crying. A nurse wearing baby blue scrubs lead me into a room and gave me grayish scrubs to put on. She had to watch me undress and feel my bra and underwear. She put my clothes and shoes in a bag and then put a metal detector around me like I was some criminal. What a warm welcome. My legs felt heavy as I walked to say goodbye to my mother and grandma. I couldn't stay here. I don't belong here. I'm okay; I'm okay. Please don't make me stay here. I kept telling my mom. She didn't want to leave me there, I could tell. But she did. With tears running down both of our faces, I watched her walk away. I went and sat on my rock-hard bed. What am I going to do? I laid there until dinner time. Garbage. It tasted terrible. It's so hard to try to think back to this day. As much as I try to think, I can't seem to remember how it went after I entered that awful place. I remember being so unhappy… I've called school "hell" for a while now. But honestly, that's as close to hell as I ever want to get. It's not necessarily that the people were unfriendly, it was just the atmosphere and my own thoughts that were driving me insane. Most of the people whom I encountered there were friendly. All of the patients that were there were nice and easy to get along with. However, there were several nurses that I was not very fond of. They did not make my stay at the hospital very much better at all. All that was on my mind was getting out of there. I had to. I didn't belong there. Although it was only a couple of hours, it felt like days walking around in my hospital scrubs. I didn't talk to anyone; it actually felt like a jail. To look out for the protected patients, anything and everything that could harm anyone in any way was removed and not allowed at the scene. For example, I use drawing as a form of relief in place of cutting. But heaven forbid me being able to draw as my drawing book had metal spirals in them and my pencils are too sharp. Now, I see why people would do this, but to me, it made my stay there even more miserable. After a never-ending race of thoughts, and piles of paperwork, I was finally given a sleeping pill and sent to lay on my hospital bed.

XXI

I was woken up at 7:00 by a nurse walking in to check my temperature and ask me to rate the physical pain that I felt on a scale of 1-10. Then I went out into the main area and had to fill out two sheets. The first one was a menu of what to eat for the day. The second was to rate your emotions. For example: Are you feeling suicidal? 1-10 Do you have anxiety? 1-10 Effectiveness of your medicine? 1-10 How did you sleep last night? And so on and so forth. Lastly, you had to set a goal for the day. The first class we went to was goals group. We basically just shared our goal and why we picked it and how it will help us grow and yada yada. Then there was a 15-minute break, and then breakfast. Although they had different names for every single transition and class, they basically all taught you the same exact thing: coping skills. Now, I was there to utilize it as a safe place, others used it as a place to learn to love themselves, deal with anger and many other more. We all respected each other for our reasons and that was simply amazing. So, being everyone was there for a different reason, you would think that there would be more one-on-one time to find the problem's root and dive deep and figure out how you can help the individual. Nope. Let's talk about the same thing for 14 hours of the day. Now, I do believe that coping skills are very important, but you don't need to talk about them every single day all the time. It's not like we are going to come up with new ones

every day. I don't know about others,
but a goal of mine was to find a coping
skill that I not only liked, but was
good at. Then I wanted to succeed at
it. I have several which I've talked
about numerous times. One, writing.
Two, drawing. Three, listening to
music. I don't see the point of having
to constantly come up with new ones. If
you're happy doing it and it works,
then keep doing it. Improve it if it's
something that can be improved. I pray
to God that you fall in love with it
and continue to do it often. That is
definitely worth more than giving up
and going through the troubles of
finding other outlets. But why would
they teach it 24/7 if it's not that
important? Beats me. Honestly, if you
want the children to get something out
of it, you need to speak to them

one-on-one. You can't put 12 kids with completely different problems together in the same room and tell them the same exact thing. It just doesn't work that way. I hope so much that the hospital changes its system. You charge so much money just to have the kid get nothing out of the experience. I do not get it at all. I guess I can't say they are totally oblivious to how to help the ones in need. Every day, we got to meet with a doctor for five minutes. Just you, him, and three other people flooding you with questions and writing everything down. Is that supposed to be helpful or productive? Maybe for the professionals. On a side note, I was already asked the same exact questions numerous times throughout my stay there. Some were to see if there was progress happening throughout my thoughts and behavior, but some were just getting so annoying. It was so overwhelming. All that I could do to get out of there was cooperate. After meeting with the doctor, I was allowed to wear my own clothes. The problem with that was, we were not allowed to have any type of strings in our clothing. Sadly, my wardrobe consists of sweatpants because I have a big butt and jeans and a big butt don't mix well. So, all of my clothes had strings in them. We just took the ones that would come out, out. They were loose, but better than wearing scrubs. I trudged on throughout the rest of the day. Something that I will not complain about at all was that a couple times a day we got to draw or paint things. I loved that. We had to all leave at the same time and go through several sets of locked doors and be escorted to a cool room where I felt more safe than any other. The even better part was that the lady that watched us was really cool and more understanding than most of the nurses. She was one of two of my favorite people there. She understood better and absorbed what I had to say and even wanted to hear so much more. It felt so great. I always looked forward to that class. Eventually, they had me giving advice to other patients. I loved it so much. It felt so good to help people. Honestly, I could see hope in the patient's eyes. It inspired me. They were coming to me for help in the group activities. That's when I really realized that I had a purpose. And my purpose is to help people. I can say it with so much confidence and it's such a great feeling. I, Camryn Nasman, have a purpose. It's just so amazing to be able to say, and be able to feel in your heart that what you're doing or thinking is right. I wanna shout it from the rooftops and tell everyone that I have a purpose. For 14 years, I wondered if I'd ever do anything great in my life. The past two years, I wondered if I would ever find an answer. For the past year and a half, I wondered why I was alive. Well, now I know. I was put on this Earth to help people through dark times. I mean, think about it. I go to a hospital for help and not even the professionals know what the hell they are doing. I'm a 14-year-old girl and I honestly and truly believe that I could have helped those kids out better than any adult there. That's kind of sad. Another point that my therapist brought up is that she has tried to understand depression for years. She's tried reading books and everything that you could think of. There's just not much out there on subjects like these. I don't know why, but people are afraid to talk about these types of things. It's not something to be embarrassed about at all. Children, adults, and everyone need to understand how these types of things really affect a person's life. This is real. Heck, I never even once got told what depression was in school. The closest thing that I ever got taught about the subject was eating disorders. That's not right. Nope, not at all. Maybe if people actually talked about this, kids wouldn't feel like such outcasts when they feel this way. Maybe we wouldn't lose so many beautiful lives to suicide. Maybe kids would be able to tell the difference between what is really their thoughts and what is the evil thing we call depression. Kids would go for help. Kids wouldn't be embarrassed. Our world would be entirely different, but for the better. My whole life I've thought it was impossible for a single person to change the world. But I sure am going to try. I can't stand by and watch kids, teenagers, adults, men and female alike; kill themselves. Is this really a world we want to live in? Think about it. I can almost guarantee that if we educated the future youth about these mental health issues, they wouldn't believe that they are messed up and alone. If we had professionals come in and teach them how to cope with the negative thoughts, or how to tell the difference between what's really theirs and what isn't, they would feel normal. I sure think that it's more important than fucking math. It will save so many lives. Since when has knowing a quadratic formula ever saved a damn life? That's what I thought. How many times has someone helping another person feel safe and whole again saved a life? Enough said. We need more life skill classes in school and not useless ones. I mean, language arts is important along with the other classes we have - if you are going to use those certain skills in life. - Otherwise, come on guys.

Back to the hospital. I hated it. I mean, I just wanted out. It wasn't helpful. As much as I wanted it to be -

gosh, I wanted it to help me so bad - it didn't. I tried so hard to get out of there. Every day, the same old thing. It honestly felt like a prison. There are 1,025,109 words in the English language, and I can't seem to string them together to tell you the atmosphere of my time in the hospital. The goal of going there was to fix me. Well, at least help my messed up mind in some way. All that I can tell you is that I wanted out. Every single day, it was a repeat of the last one. My heart was heavier and heavier every day. Walking down the hall, I felt as if I was an animal. I was trapped. I guess that there was something successful out of this. My mind was no longer set on hurting myself; it was set on getting out of there.

XXII

My first full day was the day that I got to meet the doctor. Yes, I get help! Haha, no. So, I did my normal morning routine of filling out papers and eating cardboard - er, breakfast.- Then one by one, each of the patients got to see the doctor. From all the talk, the doctor seemed to be an amazing dude. Everyone was excited, and all of the nurses seemed to swoon over him. I was pretty anxious to get the chance to talk to him. I wanted help. I went into the hospital thinking that I was going to get it. When my name was called, my emotion became more positive, and I walked down the hall accompanied by a nurse. As I walked in, the first thing I wondered was why in the world there are so many people in here. Isn't this supposed to be private? Guess not. Oh well. For starters, the guy was really hard to understand. Then they asked me the same questions over and over again. The questions didn't seem to matter. It was a depression test. I could tell, the same questions. It's a quick five or six-minute session with the "God of the hospital." They gave me the prescription for antidepressants, and an informational packet to go along with it. Before they could give me my pills, I had to memorize the name, milligrams, purposes of taking it and three side effects. I was nervous. I mean, it's not a big task, but I was still nervous. I did fine. Right away I was flooded with questions about if I felt any different. I was just shocked. Be patient. To escape all of the questions, I went and laid down in bed because that was the most entertaining thing that I could do. I felt super tired, but that was a side effect. So, I convinced myself to go tell the nurse that I was exhausted. But I fell asleep before I could even get up. I woke up about 30 minutes later. Luckily, that was during our morning break, so I didn't miss out on anything. I went and told a nurse, and they laughed and said we'd switch them to be taken at night. They asked again if I felt any different. I didn't get frustrated this time. I did notice a slight difference. I told them, "I don't know if it was the nap or not but the air feels lighter. I have less anxiety." We shared a laugh, and I gathered my supplies for the next activity.

The air felt so dense and negative as I trudged along throughout the day. My thoughts were filled with ways to get out and my heart filled with thoughts of my friends and family. The want to be back home was so strong. My emotions changed. Everything changed. I was only gone for a couple of days, but honestly, it felt like months since I've been in contact with the people that I love. For the first time since I could remember, I was missing people so bad that it hurt. I wanted to hug them so bad. I wanted to tell them how much I love them and hold them and never again take them for granted. I wanted a taste of reality. To feel alive. I needed out. Honestly, the most fun thing I could do willingly was to look out the window. That only made me so much more upset. I remember whenever seeing a Chrysler Town & Country minivan, my heart would race. I would look for the fishing stickers on the side and watch it park, praying that it was my mom to come pick me up. It never was. I spent hours watching cars and daydreaming about getting out of there. Little did I know, the day I got put into the hospital would be the last time that I cried in weeks. Looking out the window and dreaming about my mom and boyfriend jumping out of the car to come see me with big smiles on their faces. It broke my heart a little more every time that I would snap back into reality. A nurse would ask if I was alright and I'd lose my gaze from the minivan. I'm just peachy. All of the emotions piled up. I couldn't cry. No matter how hard I tried. I was a water balloon filled up all the way. Just drops away from reaching its breaking point.

Finally, something positive I can write about. So, one of my nights there, I came across a nurse that I really liked. My mom just happened to be visiting me. We are only allowed visitors over the age of 18, and they had to be immediate family members, from 5:00 pm - 7:00 pm I told the nurse how bad I wanted to leave. She gave me some major "hints" on how to get out. I took notes. I wanted out bad. I do my normal routine, and later I met with the doctor. It went very well. I told him that I was ready to leave. We talked, I told him my reasons and things that I got out of it. We talked about my medicine and he said that I could leave the next day. I wanted to cry because I was so happy! I get out. I continued to do the same things only I had a much more positive attitude, and it showed. I was much more talkative and willing to talk to patients and staff. I waited until noon so that I could call my mom and tell her the uplifting news. I was so, so excited to leave. I told her to bring my boyfriend with to come pick me up too. The day went by slowly, but that didn't matter because tomorrow I'd be sleeping in my own bed again and surrounded by the ones I love.

XXIII

The day that I got discharged wasn't what I was expecting. Maybe I just had a positive attitude because I knew that I was getting out of there. I do not exactly know. However, there was indeed a difference in my attitude. I was very talkative when before, I kept all of my thoughts and emotions to myself. I mean, yeah, I participated in group activities when I was called on or pointed at. I was not disrespectful. I just chose not to give it my all. However, May 13th was different. I found myself talking more than the instructor; I was giving the other patients advice. They liked it too. It felt so good. I was helping; making a difference in these stranger's lives. I wanted more of that. I felt like I had a use. Like I said before, that's when I really realized that I had a purpose. Helping people. I like the sound of that. I don't see anything better than helping someone through a tough time. Nothing. I'm good at it, and I liked doing it, so why not make something out of it? I think before I mentioned a guy that I had a big crush on took down the wall that depression puts up for seeing the future. John Green. I thought I liked him. Haha.

XXIV

My Gerbil

Lucas Scott Fogelberg. I've mentioned him so many times throughout my book, but I never gave him the appreciation that he deserves. So, this is where I start to write about him. We first met at state ice fishing on February 19th, 2016. I never really had any intentions of getting to know this guy. The first words he said towards me was, "I don't want to sit by Camryn, she's mean" and he had the cutest little smile on his face. I wasn't attracted to him at first. He made me laugh a lot. He rode with us in the car, and I used him as a footrest. I could tell he was starting to like me. Constantly trying to make me laugh. I thought he was very amusing, but wasn't thinking about anything romantic between us. But we continued to talk and make each other smile and laugh. I was completely oblivious to it at this point in time. I didn't realize how happy he made me. We really started to get along when we stopped at Walmart. My mom said I had to go pick out pants and he said he wanted to go with me. So, we messed around, and he helped me pick out a pair of pants. I kept complaining because there weren't any long ones; all that they had were joggers. He patiently waited for me to find a pair of pants that I liked, then we started walking away. Out of the corner of my eye, I saw a Teenage Mutant Ninja Turtle shirt on sale, and I had to get that too. He and I walked around trying to find my mom. I texted her, but she didn't answer. An idea popped into my head, and I laughed and shared it with him. "Let's do it!" So, I told him to pick out a thong and get on with it. He wouldn't, he was way too embarrassed. Then he walked past very fast and then turned around to return to me. "The green one," He had good taste in underpants. They were pretty sexy. I grabbed them, and we looked all around for my mom and the other student with her. It seemed to pop into our heads at the same time. Yep, she's at the fishing stuff. And there she was. I walked up to Noah and hung the neon green thong in the hood of his sweatshirt. Luke and I could not keep quiet. We both laughed so hard and then my mom pointed it out to Noah. I then tried to hang it on a fishing pole, but I'm only 5'3" so that didn't work out the best for me. Luke was 6'3" at the time, so he hung it up there with ease. He and I really had a good time, but for some reason, I didn't pick up on it yet. After my mom got everything she needed, she checked out and said we could Redbox a movie. Luke and I both said we wanted a scary movie. We were already picking some out, and we both got excited to watch them. Did I mention that Noah has no balls, so he basically threw a tantrum because he doesn't like scary movies? Luke and I made fun of him for a while, then we got Jurassic World for the scared little boy - he was almost 16. I continued to use Luke as a footrest, and we watched the movie. My mom made a big deal over Luke not being her friend on Facebook. So, I had to turn on my cellular data for him. He accepted her request, then I saw him go on Snapchat.

"You have Snapchat?" I said smiling.

"Yeah," Luke responded also smiling.

"What's your username?"

Then we argued over who was going to add who and I ended up adding him. Little did I know, asking for his Snapchat was the second-best thing I ever did. After hours, we finally reached the hotel. Luke and Noah helped carry bags up into our room. Moments later, Noah and I started having a pillow fight. Luke joined in too; only he kept farting and it stunk really bad. I got hit in the face and by the time I looked up, Luke was already in the bathroom. After what seemed to be forever, he came out with a big smile on his face. I had to pee, so I walked over there. Oh my goodness, did that bathroom reek! I turned on the fan and shut the door. Luke took a picture of me when was doing just that. My mom came into the room and gave the boys the key to their room. Luke was already Snapchatting me even though we just saw each other. I wasn't really excited, I was actually creeped out by it. I didn't pay any attention to it at all really. He called me cute, so I sent him a video of me farting thinking that that would repel him away. Nope. He also thought that it was cute and sent one back. I liked that. Later, Luke and Noah came into our room. Luke kept taking Snapchats of me; I didn't care. Then I got the bright idea to go swimming. Noah said he forgot his suit, but Luke has extra shorts, so he said

he was going to go. John, Jordan, and
Bryanna also went swimming. Bryanna
didn't go swimming for long, but
everyone else did. Unlike a normal
person, Luke did a front flip into the
pool. Bryanna and I slowly made our way
in. So did John. When Luke did a flip,
I almost had a heart attack because it
looked like he was going to smack his
head on the side of the pool. He was
alright, and I took a sigh of relief.
We all messed around then Bryanna left.
John kept getting really close and
picking me up and moving me around in
the water. Luke would go after me, and
then they'd both throw me. Once, my
bottoms of my swimsuit came off. Jordan
was behind me.

"Did you see my butt?" I screamed
at him. Also, the first words I said to
him.

"No." He said with confidence.

We all messed around, and it was an amazing experience. We splashed each other, and I kept getting thrown into the water. I was swimming away from Luke and John because they kept picking me up. Jordan was at the end of the pool that I was swimming towards. I knew who he was, we just never had a conversation. Jordan then decides that it would be an amazing idea to body slam me. After almost dying on several occasions, we all settled down. Jordan left so it was just me, Luke and John. We had a pretty good conversation, and we told stories to each other. The whole time, John was holding me. Luke was getting jealous, and it was evident. I didn't care at all, though. I didn't like him. We all sat and talked for about an hour. It was getting late, and the pool was going to close soon, so we got up and dried off. We all went back to our rooms. John came in later. I also asked for his Snapchat. I then tried to show John how to make Dubsmashes. John returned to his room, and I Snapchatted Luke, Noah, and John. I was mostly focused on John. I was starting to develop a crush on him.

The next day we headed out to the lake to go fishing. I didn't get to go fishing, though. I was an Eighth grader at the time, so I didn't get to fish otherwise it'd be against the rules. That didn't stop me from going. For some reason, I had a huge feeling that I needed to go. I was originally going to hang out with my friend Sage but I canceled. I now know why. The fishing was very slow. I was helping John set up tip ups and mostly hanging out with him. We were flirting with each other a lot. After a lot of talking, he was getting tired so he went to sleep in the car. Luke and Noah invited me to go into the shack with them. Luke and I had an ice fight. We are both so immature. Then we all got bored and went outside. The ice was melting, and there was legit a foot of water on the ice. We started messing around. Noah and I tried to hit Luke with a rubber band we found on the ice. It was difficult because we were against the wind. After numerous tries, I went again, only to break the rubber band and for it to fall into a hole. At almost the same moment it landed, it sunk to the bottom. At the time, it was the funniest thing in the world. Later we found a board on the ice and pretended it was a skateboard. The ice was extra slippery from the water, and it was hilarious. To our surprise, none of us slipped yet. After that, we played soccer with the wooden board. I was having so much fun. Noah went back to fish, and Luke watched as I went on my imaginary skateboard. Just my luck, I flipped over on the ice. I got soaked. We both laughed so hard. I had so much fun that weekend. The trip home was fun too. After the fishing trip, we stayed in touch. We have talked every single day since then. I started to catch feelings for Luke. But at the time, I was going to try to make it work with John. So, I didn't tell him I thought he was super cute, or flirt with him. In my mind, I couldn't like him. So, that's what I did, only it didn't work.

I saw Luke at school a lot. I didn't talk to him much. He knew that I liked John, but he still continued to call me beautiful every day. When something went wrong, Luke was there. Literally. When I was sad, he would rush over. Once, I was crying over John, and I had the urge to cut. I was talking to Luke and - I mentioned this before- we talked for 13 hours straight. That was the day I let go of John. I really liked Luke. This man didn't give up even though I was giving all of my attention to someone else. If I ever fell down, he was right there to pick me up. After numerous times of hanging out, I was ready to date him. Earlier I said that the second-best thing I have ever done in my life was asking for his Snapchat. The first was saying yes to being his girlfriend. I can't begin to tell you how lucky I am to have someone to support me through such tough times. If you have someone that supports you and loves you unconditionally through a rough patch, you better be grateful. There are a lot of people who don't have that kind of support system. This man came into my life unexpectedly, and I couldn't be happier about it. If you have relationship anxiety, you know how absolutely terrible it is. Mine wasn't so much, "oh, he's cheating on me, or, he doesn't really like me" it was, "you don't even like him." I hated it so much. I knew I liked him. But it's so difficult when you're your own worst enemy, and it's you saying these things. What it was, was me, wrapping myself in like a bubble wrap. It kept me from feeling too sad and feeling too

happy. I was numb. It's why I started
cutting again. I felt nothing. I had to
feel something again. My mind wouldn't
let me believe that someone so amazing
could actually want me. I would just
get hurt again. I couldn't handle
another heartbreak. And I knew that.
So, I shut him down. But Luke didn't
give up. He waited three months. Three
months, to call me his. I'm so grateful
he didn't give up. He has helped me so
much. There are times where I'm a total
bitch, and he just holds me. He knows
when it's me and when it isn't. I have
more moments where I feel like my old
self again; the happy one. When I'm
having a panic attack, and push him
away, he is just more determined to
help. He can always put a smile on my
face no matter what. He is so important
to me. I give him the power to take

everything away from me. Because he is my everything. But he's helped me through so much; I can't ever let him go. Thank you so much. I wouldn't be here without you. I mean it when I say, don't take anyone for granted. If they try to help you, let them. The saying, "you never know what you have until it's gone." is entirely true. I learned the hard way. Trust me, hold on tight and show the people around you some appreciation. The ones who are by your side are affected too. Don't forget that.

Before, I thought that John took down the wall for me. Good one. Luke completely took down my wall. I am thinking about what I am going to do as a career, where I want to go to school, where I want to work, where I want to live and how I am going to raise my children. I honestly could never thank him enough for always being my rock. I really do believe that I am in love with him. I would do anything for him, honest. I would. I would spend forever with him. I've never felt this way about anyone else. I thought a lot about my future. All thanks to Luke. It felt so good. I actually told my friend Seth about it. We were talking about if children should be able to be transgender or if I would let my kid be gay. This is what was said,

"Pretty much. Whatever makes them happy."

"That's the way to do it."

"My kid is going to know they're loved and supported. But still not spoiled."

"That's a good way to go into things."

"It's true. I am going to make sure they know it, too. Every day and every night I am going to tell them how beautiful, smart and important they are. So they grow up knowing it and never forget it."

Then he said he wanted to hear more of what I thought about my future. I felt like I was talking way too much, but he said he was okay with it.

"I'm thinking about my future - I really like thinking about my future- and how I can change people for the better in the future. That's how I believe that it should always be. My kids are going to know they are important. I am not going to keep anything from them. They'll know the world is a shitty place, but I will show them how to get through it because they're beautiful and so important.

They will know their worth, and I'm happy about that."

Then he wanted to hear more. I didn't know what else to talk about, so I just told him career wise what my plans were.

"Well, my plans for high school is to do whatever and not really give a shit about other people's opinions. See where grades get me. I want to get out of this small town. I want to travel. Go to some school for four - eight years. During that time, I would be getting paid to help people. AWESOME. While also learning how to do a better job of helping people. They say, 'Find a job you love and you'll never work a day in your life.' That's what I think about this. I love helping people and do it now, so why not do it as a career, and get paid for it too? That's a bonus. After I get all of my schooling and hours done, I would be a self-employed psychologist. By then I will have my book published and who knows, maybe I'll even go a different path just from that. As long as I make a difference and I am happy, I'm good. I'm set on helping people."

Seth was very proud of me for thinking and planning for my future. I was too. It doesn't happen often. He still wanted to hear more. So, I told him that I was planning to live close to a town but not in town. Not sure about the city or state yet, but I have time to plan. Yet he still wanted to hear more. So, I told him more about how I would raise my kids.

"I really am going to treat my kids like a prince or princess. I want at least two. I mean it when I say I am going to tell them every single day how important they are. They will be my world. I will tell them every night how beautiful they are, how smart they are, how perfect they are. They will believe it too. They will believe they are worth something because they are. I will always show them how much I love them. Not by giving them what they want, like a new toy or new movie. No. I will tell them stories. Not about princesses that live happily ever after. No. There will be ones with bad endings. I will show them that life isn't fair at a young age. I will prepare them for the truth. I will not build a perfect bubble like Disney movies do. My kids will know the truth. The stories that I tell, well, they will probably be disappointed with them. But they can't have this false belief in everything always ends up okay. I am also going to encourage them always to go for their dreams. They will have a positive outlook; I will show them the good in things. They will already know that life isn't fair, well, they will have the idea of it. They probably won't truly believe it until something bad happens to them, locking the idea into place. My kids will know about my past and not want their future to be the same. My kids will use manners toward everyone for they will be aware that everyone has a story and you don't know it. Always be kind. Say hi to the kid that sits alone, offer a piece of gum to the kid everyone calls a nobody. Be a voice for the voiceless. Those little things build character, and I want my kids to know that. I will teach them everything

I know about being a good person because, in the end, that is so important. They will know that they are perfect in my eyes. We will have a close relationship. I won't judge them, and I will always be here to support them."

I told him that I only really thought about my future with my kids and career. That was a lie, though. I was constantly thinking about my future. Maybe not about what kind of car I want or how I am going to dress, but who is going to be in my life that far ahead on the road. When I look into my future, all I see is Luke. Not going to lie. I see us being together forever. It is so clear. I hope it's true. I always thought that we would be, until August 15th. I swear to God I never experienced so much pain in my life. I would have rather been dead than feel what I felt that day.

I have a lot of issues you have noticed. Most of the time, I can't help it. I sometimes seem to forget how much he actually does for me. I've gotten so much better during my time with him. I have put him through so many situations where he could have just got up and left but instead, he stayed. He's stayed by my side through thick and thin. I have so many flaws, imperfections, and reasons not to love me. Yet the perfect person chooses to be with me. I will never understand why, but I am so glad that he looks past all of my imperfections and still loves me. You know why? Because he means the entire world to me. When he is gone, I crave him in my arms. When he is with me, I never want to let him go. I see him in my future, and I have no intentions of never letting him go. I would give him everything I have to make him happy. But the truth is, he is actually everything I have. Just the thought of losing you hurts me. I couldn't stand walking past you in the halls, making awkward eye contact, because we were strangers again. I couldn't take it. I know that you mean the entire world to me.

You're so amazing, Luke. I never want you to think badly about yourself. You are so important and so loved. You make me so happy. There are so many reasons to fall in love with you. You're perfect. Honestly, in my eyes, you're perfect. I can't lie. I wouldn't want to be with anyone else. You're hardworking, strong, and determined. You don't give up easily. You work towards what you want until you get it. That's a great trait to have. You're caring, kind and outgoing. You are so important to me. I know sometimes I overreact and you may not feel as special. I'm so sorry. You're my king. And I'm going to treat you like one because you deserve it. You're special and worth so much.

Your happiness is my happiness. Just know, I never want to make you upset. I'm sorry. I am stupid and say things I don't mean sometimes. I get super jealous, easy. You know that. I can't stand the thought of you being with someone else. My goal is to make you fall in love with yourself. It's so easy to love you, I want you to do the same. My goal is to make you the happiest man in the world. It won't be easy because I'm a ding a ling, but I promise I will try. It's my job to make you feel special, and you damn better expect me to try. I love you. And you better always feel loved. If you ever don't, tell me. I love you so much. Don't forget it. Ever.

You mean the world to me and I know you always will. If I lost you, I would lose everything, because you are my everything. Please, never let us not be together. I cannot see my future without you in it. I want us to live in our own house. Waking up to each other and watching SpongeBob in our underwear. There are days I'll make a big breakfast, and there are days we will eat cereal like we would do when we were teenagers. Just you and me; no one to tell us to be quiet. Because it's us.

I didn't realize how attached I really was until the 15th of August. He broke up with me. He gave up. I can't say I didn't deserve it. I did give him everything that I had to offer. I also am messed up. He doesn't understand, though. Anxiety has a mind of its own. It has major jealousy involved. Now, I was the jealous type before, but with anxiety, you can only imagine the monster I turn into. So, even if Luke talks to another girl or likes another girl's picture, I get sad. I don't go crazy on him. I usually keep the reason I am upset to myself. But that doesn't stop me from taking my anger out on him. I would take it all back, if I could. The underappreciating. I mean, I said thank you all the time to him, but I never really felt it. I never looked at what he did for me and truly was thankful. You have to look deeper into things than just, "He never buys me flowers. He plays too many video games." Instead, look at it like, "He always makes me smile when I'm sad. He looks so cute when he's focused on something." That little change in mindset could save a relationship. Honestly, you hear, "Look at the positive side." A lot. It gets tiring after a while, but it is so true. Just the simple change in the way you think and it opens a whole new world. Trust me on this. Positive thinking is key. My mom has told me that from day one. I never took it to heart and always found it annoying when she said it. But after going through hell, I realized that she was right this whole time. Turn the situation around.

It was late at night and I was overreacting over a stupid thing again with Luke. I really do have a problem with saying stuff I don't mean. For some odd reason, I always say, "We should break up," out of nowhere. I have never meant it once out of all the times that I have said it. I've said it before and I'll say it again; I love him. I wouldn't give up on him. I think it's my way of getting reassured maybe. I run away and he chases back. I think that it was my sure way of knowing he still wanted me… For him to never let me leave, and I loved it. I loved when he didn't want me to leave. That's when he would show me how much I meant to him. He wasn't the best with his words, but he sure made me feel loved when I tried to break up with him. Call me a bad person, I don't care. I just wanted to know how much he really cared for me. I knew it was wrong and slowed down on it a lot, especially when I started taking my pills again. No one deserves to have their emotions toyed with like that. I was inconsiderate to how it was affecting his emotions and thoughts. If I could go back in time and change the way I acted and treated him, I would in a heartbeat. So, I begged for him to stay. I gave it my all.

Once he told me that he wanted to break up, I felt like my heart just got hit by an eighteen-wheeler. My mom happened to just go in and check on me. Before he said he didn't want to be with me anymore, I had my sharpest blade in my hand and tears in my eyes. I was just about to skype my friend Rilee when Luke informed me that I was no longer his. I kept yelling at my mom and telling her to get out and leave me alone. She didn't obey. She couldn't leave me alone, I was a suicidal mess. Who would leave me alone? I hit my head against the wall a couple times and then ran outside barefoot. I never cried like this before. I've had my heart broken several times, but this one was just so different. It hurt much more than anything I have ever experienced. I basically was screaming. I was begging for him not to leave but he kept making excuses. The one person that I thought would be with me forever, gave up. For some odd reason, I believed Luke. I actually thought he meant it when he said that he wanted to be together forever. I thought that he meant it when he said he would love me even on my bad days, and that he could handle my disorders because he loved me. But I made the stupid decision to fall into every word he said. I am not trusting of people at all. I have been walked over so many times, believing people without hesitation would be stupid on my part. For Luke, I thought that maybe I was sent something amazing because I needed something amazing. Maybe all of the bullshit I have been through lead me up to the love of my life. That's what I saw it as. He was going to be mine forever and I was going to be his. Then one day out of nowhere, he decides that I am not good enough to keep fighting for. It killed me. Never did I ever think for one second that he would leave me. I believed it when he said that I was the love of his life. Yeah, I am young, but true love doesn't meet you at your best, it meets you in your mess. I pray that that's my mess. Because, that was such a rough time for me when I met him. I never knew that he would end up meaning so much to me. He was my world, my everything, and I really thought that I was in love. Of course, there are a lot of teenagers who date someone for five minutes and call what they have, "love." However, I have said I love you and not meant it to people. But with Luke, it was different. I felt like he was a part of me. When he was gone, I craved his presence. I guess that I should not have gotten attached. I should not have fallen so hard for his beautiful blue eyes and his craziness equal to mine. But, it wasn't my choice. He is perfect in my eyes. Me trying not to fall in love with him wouldn't have made any difference. He is perfect in my eyes. By perfect, I don't mean that he doesn't have any flaws. Sometimes his farts are a little too strong and his breath stinks. But it's more reason to fall in love with him. He is perfect for me. He is my everything and his giving up on us doesn't change that. I couldn't put into words the amount of pain I felt when he said we should break up. I wasn't enough. All of the times that he said he never would give up, he lied. I let him in, and he destroyed me. Nothing in the world hurt more than him leaving. I always gave this piece of advice to people; "Never let your happiness depend on another person." It is hard sometimes, but true. You can love someone with all of your heart, but you can't let them be the only thing that you love. When or if they leave, what do you have? In your eyes, nothing. You have nothing. You feel empty and worthless. But beautiful, that's not the case at all. You just put all of your love and priorities into this one person. You can't let everything depend on one person, because then if you lose them, you feel so empty. I find it really weird because I always said that to people, yet I did exactly the opposite. Luke is my everything. I would do anything to see his cute smile or hear the laugh that he hates, but I completely adore. Anything. When Luke gave up, I thought of all of the things I could have changed. I thought that I treated him pretty good, but I could do better. Less meaningless arguments, less complaining. More laughs, more "I appreciate you's. If you are reading this, and you are in a happy relationship, takes these words into consideration. Alright, if you take a moment and imagine your future, do you see your boyfriend/girlfriend in it? If you do, great. Now, imagine not having them in your life anymore. Just think of seeing them while walking down the street, making awkward eye contact, and remembering the times you had together. Do you want that? If not, take my advice. If your person doesn't like you talking to that one chick or dude, but you still do, stop. Do you want to give up a temporary "friend," for someone you see in your future? No. If your boyfriend doesn't like when you show off your boobs on Snapchat, don't do it. If your girlfriend hates when you like other girl's selfies, or comment on them, don't do it. Seriously guys, it's not that hard. In today's world, relationships are lucky to last two weeks. You know how when you first start dating someone and you have the butterflies and the lovey-dovey stuff? That fades. That's not what being in love is. It's not the constant in love feeling and being all over each other. But that's what kind of belief is in the young people's heads. Movies promote happy endings. They show us that life is a fairy tale. It shows us that there's always a happy ending, which there isn't. Life is so unfair, guys. A relationship isn't perfect. It never will be overall. So when something goes wrong, people automatically think, "This isn't perfect so this isn't the person for me," which isn't true. Life just isn't easy and neither are relationships. If you think that the individual of your dreams is just going to come to you without effort, you're on some next level poop. A relationship takes work. It takes change and commitment. If you think you're in some fairy tale, you're wrong. Life is so, so unfair. I can't stress enough how life isn't easy. But if you want to have a long-lasting relationship, you need to understand everything behind it. It's more than just taking cute pictures together and holding hands. Are you going to be there for them when their pet or family member dies, are you going to be there to celebrate when they get accepted into college? If they call at 3:00am crying, will you help, or give up because it's too much? If you want something real, you have to fight for it. Love is worth fighting for. The real stuff, is difficult and ugly, but overall it is the most beautiful thing in this world. Being connected to another human being, sharing the same stories and having someone else's happiness be your happiness, that is truly beautiful. But are you going to fight for it? Are you going to fix what is broken and grow as a couple? Go tell your person that you are grateful for them. Tell them thank you for everything they do for you because you never know when it can all be taken away from you. Make them feel appreciated and good about themselves.

My heart burns. I feel like it is physically burning. I miss him... I do more than anything. I would do anything to go back in time. Really, I would. I keep skyping my friend Rilee because he really helps take my mind off of things. He really makes me laugh, he helps me a lot. If it weren't for him, I don't know how I would have survived. He distracted me a lot. So, when he'd ask to skype I would forget all of my worries and be happy. I didn't even think of Luke when I talked to him, which was amazing. I've known Rilee for about a year now, but only became close when we started working together. He was a really good friend. Seriously, one of my number one supporters, he helped me a lot. So, we became closer. I loved skyping him, it was all making jokes and laughing. I was glad I had something in my life to take away the pain. It was sort of like how some people would drink, smoke, or cut. But I talked to him. But at 3:00 when he would fall asleep, and I was left alone again, Luke flooded my thoughts. I literally stayed up crying until 6:00

am almost every night after we broke up. I'm not a religious person, so I don't pray every night or go to church at all. I do, however, believe that there's a higher power. I'm not sure of my religion, but as the tears rolled down my face and my heart ached, I prayed. For the second time in my life, I prayed. I prayed for Luke. I kept saying, "Please, I need him. I will treat him better, please, please. I don't know what I will do without him, I need him. I want him in my life, I won't take him for granted please. I love him. I never ask you for anything, please, hear me out, please." Stuff like that. I said it aloud, in the most heartbreaking voice. Seriously, it hurt my own heart even more to hear myself so upset. The hot tears felt like poison, leaving my eyes with such burning sensation it hurt to keep them open. But it also hurt my heart to close them because all that I saw was Luke. It hurt to swallow. I felt like I was chugging down a thick substance of all of my mistakes. All I could do was pray, cry, and feel pure pain. After basically begging for him to stay, I decided not to text him anymore. It was so hard. I always caught myself going into our conversation and wanting to type, "Hey babe. I love you and have a great day!" But I couldn't. It didn't take long for me to break the promise to myself and text him. He put something sad on his Snapchat story, so I asked if he was okay. It wasn't the same. The way that he talked to me was so different. He didn't want anything to do with me anymore. I could tell by his words. It fucking hurt. If I could somehow grasp together the right words to tell you how bad it hurt, I am not sure I would want to. I mean, of course, an author loves putting the reader in the situation, but I don't ever, ever want anyone to feel what I felt when I lost him. I wouldn't even wish the pain on my worst enemy. Later, I convinced him to let me call him. I was feeling good about it. Maybe I could show him how much he meant to me. I called and quickly ended it because I was having trouble breathing. Phone calls aren't a walk in the park for me. I built up my courage once again and clicked his contact. Here we go. So, we started off and it was super awkward. There wasn't any emotion in his voice at all. It was so weird to hear him like that. Now, his reasoning for breaking up was because he kept hurting me. That was probably the stupidest thing that I have ever heard in my life. Luke helped me more than anyone else in the world, and to hear him say that, was ridiculous. I mean, the time he called me fat when he didn't mean it, hurt a little, but I obviously got over it. Not once in our entire relationship, have we had an argument or situation worth giving up over. Never, not once. I poured my heart out to him. Honestly, I told him how important he was and how I care about him. I gave him so many reasons not to give up. Literally, if I wrote our conversation down, and gave it to my teacher as an argumentative essay, I would have gotten an A+. Easily my best convincing, in my opinion. But it wasn't enough for Luke, I guess. I tired myself out giving the facts that

I did. He said he still loved me, but when I asked him why he didn't want to be together, he'd say, "I do, but I can't keep hurting you." Which was super dumb in my opinion. I literally sat on the phone with him for over an hour, and I felt as if I gave him a million reasons on why we shouldn't give up. Honestly, you would be surprised how hard I fought to get him back. It was almost like he muted me the entire phone call; he didn't budge at all. I was so tired and gave it my all. If someone doesn't want me in their life this much, why keep fighting? There is nothing more that I could have said. I just simply gave up. Just like that. I was in tears when I said, "Okay, you clearly don't want me in your life. You wouldn't keep making bullshit excuses and would actually consider what I am saying if you did. I'm done fighting for someone that doesn't want me, goodbye." Then he said, "No," as I hung up. It really was shocking that I said that. I asked Rilee if we could skype so I didn't have a total breakdown, he always helped me. I explained to him what happened and he made me feel so much better. He told me that I deserve better, which I didn't believe because in my mind, Luke was the best. But from the outside, he said Luke didn't think of me as anything above average. Rilee explained how so many guys, like himself, think I am absolutely amazing. Which is true actually. Why be looked at as average when the right guy will find you perfect? Rilee helped me so much. He is the reason it stopped hurting less. He is the reason I didn't do anything stupid in such a difficult situation. Rilee helped me a lot. I am glad. It hurt so bad without Luke, but Rilee took a lot of pain away. It still didn't stop it from hurting. Whenever Luke showed up in my newsfeed on Facebook, or I had to go through my photos to find an old picture, I would see his name or his cute little face. It hurt, it really did. I always thought Luke was the missing piece to my puzzle. Gosh, he is so important to me. Yes, he still is, even though he dumped me and even though he doesn't want me in his life anymore. I still love him the same. The feelings don't just go away when you get out of a relationship. I meant everything I said to him, even though he didn't. I still respect him the same and I still am going to keep all of his secrets and dreams to myself. Just because he left, doesn't mean anything is gone. He is still Luke. He isn't mine anymore, but he is still the same person that I am in love with. So why try and ruin his life, or make things worse? That's the problem with people these days. They take a breakup as a form of vengeance. It shouldn't be that way. Just because someone breaks you, doesn't mean you have to break them back. That does not fix you. No, it makes things worse. A lot of teenagers and adults think that just because you aren't dating that person, all of a sudden, you don't love them and you have to hate them. No. Well, if they cheated on you, disrespected you, abused you, then you have a reason to dislike them. But still, don't be petty. You can dislike them, just don't try and ruin them. It makes things worse for the both of you. You almost all of the time should still have feelings for them. I mean, are they just going to vanish into thin air? No. They are still there, and if they aren't, they never existed in the first place. It is normal to have a hard time with a breakup and to still care and to still have feelings for your ex. It is hard, guys. Really, really, hard. I honestly didn't think I could make it without Luke. But, I started looking on the positive side of things. For one, I can talk to whoever I want now. All the guys that I stopped talking to for Luke, we can talk again. That's not much, but maybe it'll make me feel better I don't know. For two, if it was meant to last, it would have. Who knows, perhaps in a few years our paths will cross again. I wouldn't mind that at all. As a matter of fact, I would love to reconnect with the man I thought was my forever. I would love for him to realize that he actually meant everything he said, he loved me and couldn't live without me. I wish that he missed me. Maybe I wouldn't feel so empty. Maybe I would feel whole again. I don't want to say I need him, because I don't. I have finally convinced myself that I don't need him. You know what they say, there's a difference in what you need, and what you want. Let's be real, I wanted Luke more than anything. I thought that I needed him, but I am still breathing so I obviously don't. I do want him. I am still staying up until 6:00am every single day. It's not even been a week yet. No talking. He seems to be taking the breakup well, which kills me. Every time I fall asleep - and you better believe me when I say this- I have a dream that Luke realized that he stills wants to be with me. Literally, every single night I dream that he comes back and everything goes back to normal. It feels so real, until I wake up. Then the only thing that I am left with is a heavy heart and hot tears stinging in my eyes. I was so, so lost. I tried to play it out as I was happy. Heck, I even made my own YouTube channel. I always smiled in my new selfies or put an inspirational quote. I couldn't give anyone the satisfaction that I was torn. I couldn't. I mean, that's what they want, isn't it? They want to see me suffer, so I didn't let them see. I put on a show. I made new videos, but had to crop so much out because I kept finding myself talking about the one that got away. All that I did was smile when I spoke about him. Stupid, because my heart is broken, but he could mend it in an instant. I missed his lips on mine, heck I even missed his farts in my face. I missed him. I never, ever missed anyone as much as I missed Luke. Never that I recall. I am trying so hard to think of a time that I was so miserable and unhappy, but I can't. I never wanted to be dead more. For real. I wasn't planning on dying this time though. No. It wasn't an option. I mean, I have a purpose, right? I need to finish this book and be a psychologist. I need to pass what I know and what I have been through to others. I need to make a difference. I need to. That's exactly what I am going to do.

Most girls, when upset, will go on social media and find a sad quote in under two minutes. I usually do that; not gonna lie, haha. But I was just sharing my normal stuff on facebook. Nothing was depressing or anything. So, it was a Thursday, I shared a thing that said, "If you think that I don't like you, like this." I was kind of shocked by the amount of people who liked it. I mean, I am not mean to people or anything. I didn't think that I gave them a reason to believe I didn't like them. Actually, I did dislike two individuals who liked the photo. Anyways, Luke liked it. Luke and I didn't like each other's stuff once we broke up at all. So, me being stupid, texted him.

I said, "I don't dislike you. *smiley face*."

Awhile later a got a response. Luke said, "Do you still like me?"

"Why?"

"Just wondering."

"Okay.'

"Okay, and?"

My heart was racing. I honestly didn't know what to say. Should I tell him the truth, or will I seem desperate? I was so confused. Should I play it cool - act like I don't care? I honestly didn't know. I was going to ask a couple of my friends for advice, but either they weren't answering, or they'd say, "Idk it's whatever you want. It's up to you." What great advice. So, I took a deep breath and typed "Yeah." Hmm. Should I send it? No. I deleted it and found myself typing yet again, and without hesitation, I hit send.

"Yeah."

Oh my gosh, what did I just do? I am stupid. Stupid, stupid, stupid. Now he is going to think I am desperate. Now he is going to know that I miss him. Now he is going to know he still has power and control over the situation. But, that's okay. Life is too short to leave important words unsaid, right? Whatever happens, is supposed to happen. Might as well take a chance or two.

"Okay and I'm sorry," he replied.

"It's okay; I'm over the breakup."

Okay, this was true. I didn't mean I didn't like him anymore. My heart just wasn't constantly craving Luke. It didn't hurt as bad. That's what I meant.

"You are? And are you over me?"

"No, I'm not over you. You don't just stop having feelings for someone."

"I know, it hurts every night I lay in bed and think about you. It hurts so much, and I don't think that I'll ever get over you."

At this point, I was speechless. I didn't know if he was getting at that he wanted to be together or what. I was a little happy to hear that he missed me, though.

"I know. I do the same. I try to distract myself, but I'm in love with you."

"I know how you feel and I am still in love with you."

"I'm sorry."

"Don't apologize, none of this was your fault."

"I just wish things would have worked out."

"I do too, and I still want them to."

Now, all that I said was, "Really?" but you can bet your buns that just that little line, erased all of the pain. At that moment, all I felt was perfect, and pure happiness and love. Honestly, everything felt at ease. But that's not all; I was crying. I was crying tears of joy. Maybe he meant it when he told me that he loved me. Maybe he really can't live without me.

"Like us to work out back to how it was." Luke replied.

I didn't really get this completely, but took a guess.

"I wish it was."

"We still can, please."

"Do you think it's a good idea?"

"Yes, so we don't have to be miserable."

"Do you regret breaking up?'

"Yes, a lot."

"Alright."

"Can we?"

The conversation went on. I told him I wanted to think about it even though I don't think anyone could have altered my decision. I was so happy. He missed me and wanted me back. I don't know; maybe he was just lonely. Maybe he just missed having someone to make him feel good about himself. Or maybe he really did think that he was missing out. Maybe he realized that I would do anything for him and he was stupid for letting go. The next day, I got up, got dressed, and Luke picked me up. We talked a bit and went to his house. Then we made out and stuff. He asked me to be his girlfriend. Then he got called into work and said I am going with. When we finally got there, you would never guess whom I saw. Go ahead. Take a wild guess. If you get it, give yourself a high five. Ready, drum roll, please… And the answer to the million dollar question is; John Green. It was awkward. The two guys I thought that I loved talking to each other. Then John dropped his water bottle and didn't even notice. Everyone was telling him, but he kept walking. I picked it up and said his name. Then he turned around. I smiled and handed it to him. He smiled back and said thank you. I followed Luke inside. I waited in the waiting area by myself. John kept looking at me, and I tried not to pay attention. Then my love came out and took me to a suburban. We went to Shell Lake to fill up propane tanks, then returned. After that long experience, we waited at Kwik Trip. Then went down the Highway about ten miles because a friend of his wanted to go look at his truck. It was boring. I kept asking myself, is this what I want? Of course it is. How devastated was I without Luke? Or was it just the feeling of being rejected? After hours of driving around and waiting, I convinced Luke to let me get us subway. So, I spent $17 on some grub, and he drove us to the lake. We ate there and laughed and smiled. We really connected. After that, we walked over to the Veterans Memorial and looked at all of the names and the statues. We both highly respect the amazing men and women that fight for our country. We looked at the soldier statues and just as we walked over to one, a giant spider crawled out of his nose! I hate spiders. Once, at 2:00am I went to let my dogs out, and Luke was over. I was trapped because there was a spider over the door. I called for Luke. I gave him the gun and made him shoot it. Funniest thing ever. So, I felt safe with him until he ran away like a little girl. Then I was scared. We laughed it off and went to my house. Then we made some Musical.lys, and he got invited to a party, so he left. Overall, it was a pretty good day. Sure, we didn't do much, but I had so much fun just being with him. I felt like me again. I was fixed. Well, scratch that. I wasn't fixed. Sure, I wasn't sad anymore. But, there's now a big part of me that doesn't believe Luke when he tells me that he loves me.

In ten days, it will be our six month anniversary. We are so happy together. Everything is going well. We have been doing more things as a couple and talking more. We explained our feelings and are willing to help them grow. This is just one of the times that I will mention Luke. Hopefully, we will last. He means a lot to me.

XXV

My hero

Finally, I can write to you something absolutely amazing. So, if you want to know more about me, besides the mental health aspect, I'll tell you. Let's see, for starters, I'm one of the funniest people that you would ever meet. I love making people laugh, and I'm pretty good at it, too. It's another form of helping people. If I can make them laugh, I'm good. I don't really show that part of me in here because it's all serious most of the time, but I'm pretty funny. I love, and I mean love, to ride four-wheelers a lot. I do some tricks, and it really clears my mind. I'm constantly smiling and laughing when I'm driving, and that's most likely because, "Oh shit, I probably should have crashed there," happens a lot. I have had a lot of accidents, but that doesn't stop me. I absolutely love fishing too. My family has a cabin near Lake of the Woods, Minnesota. I love adventuring. I've found several old cars and parts of cars in my woods, and I love that. I want to travel and see new places when I'm older. I want to try new things. I love playing sports, too. My favorites are softball and volleyball. With depression, I lost my drive and motivation for a while, but I'm getting it back. Obviously, I love writing. I love singing even though a cat getting laid sounds better than me. I like learning new things. I know several songs on guitar and piano just from YouTube videos. I love drawing so much, and I love scary movies. I have two dogs, and one bunny. I love animals. I have a lot of different breeds of dogs on my bucket list. Instead of being the crazy cat lady, I will be the crazy dog lady. Maddie is three years old and Bella is seven. I just got Charlie this summer at the fair. Anyways, there's a lot more to me, but I am just gonna get to the chase. Okay, so since I was a little girl, I've been obsessed with football. I love it. Watching it, playing it, whatever. I just love football. If you personally know me, you would know that I'm a HUGE fan of the Minnesota Vikings. My favorite person in the entire world is Blair Walsh. I've had a crush on him for two years and looked up to him for the same amount of time. I've always jokingly stated that I was going to marry him, and I would put him as my MCM on Instagram. Everyone went along with it, and life was great. I've lived in Wisconsin my entire life so you can only imagine how much shit I get thrown at me for that. Packer fans are seriously the worst. Most of them anyways. Some are nice, but most that I know will verbally or physically do stuff to ruin your day. For example, if you are a Vikings fan and you go to Lambeau Field, the Packer fans would seriously dump drinks on you. With that said, we don't go to Green Bay to watch any games anymore. Not all fans are like that, just a lot. Once, someone was making fun of Blair Walsh. This was two years ago, so before he missed the game-winning field goal against Seattle. My friends at lunch were just like, "Oh, Blair Walsh sucks," and this

and that. I turned around and said, "I
would shut up before Blair Walsh comes
around and kicks your balls 70 yards."
Let's just say they shut right up after
that. Anyways, I'm a huge Viking fan
win or lose. Always have, always will.
We've started a tradition of going to
their training camp. I always have so
much fun there. July 31st, 2016, I got
to go for the second year. The first
year was absolutely amazing. Here's
what made it amazing: right when we
walked in, I saw Blair Walsh on the
field. I know, simply amazing. It got
awkward because we were making eye
contact for about 25-30 seconds. I
built up the courage to wave at him. He
smiled and waved back. I froze. I
literally froze in the middle of the
walking area, with my mouth wide open,
and started crying. Yuck. I felt like

an annoying fangirl, but I guess that I was. No one knew why in the hell I was crying, and I really didn't either, but it goes to show how much I like Blair Walsh. Everyone kept trying to get his autograph, but all that I wanted was a picture. I would rather have a picture with him than an autograph any day. After a very fun day, it was time to go. I wasn't giving up that easily. I waited 30 minutes at the gates after closing time, and I met just about every single player besides Blair. Oh well. "Next year," I told myself. So, yeah, July 31st, let's hope that I get to meet Blair Walsh.

Hey, guys, training camp was really fun. I didn't get to meet Blair Walsh, but I have a fun story to tell you guys. They had a booth set up where you can write to your favorite player, and of course, I wrote to Blair Walsh. I've been meaning to write about him for a long time because really, he was a big part of my recovery. I mentioned the missed field goal earlier in this chapter. If you don't already know, Blair Walsh had the opportunity to bring the Vikings closer to the Super Bowl. It was only 27 yards. All of the pressure was on him. He gets ready, the whole time I say, "Come on, Blair, you got this. I believe in you." Quietly to myself. He kicked, and totally shanked it wide left. Me, being his number one fan, punched the floor and ran outside. You can't be totally mad at Blair. Sure, he missed, but he was also the only reason we had the chance to win. He put all of the points on the board. Zero of it was from the offense. So, I wasn't mad for long. I immediately started to stand up for him. People were being such assholes, and I wouldn't have it. I did my best to stand up for him. For two weeks straight, this really annoying guy reminded me of it every single morning. I stood up for Blair every time I heard him being spoken of in a bad way. How was Blair handling it? Well, like a champ. I've never seen such a positive attitude in my life. I was really proud of him. If I were in that situation, I have no idea what I would do. If I miss a shot at basketball practice, I think about it for a long time and feel guilty; I can't even imagine how he felt. But Blair, he was so positive about it, and he moved forward. I was inspired. That's kind of when I started thinking like wow, people's opinions really don't matter. It seemed as if the entire world is against him, and there he is, confident and ready for the next season. Blair has always been my role model. He's more than just a guy who can kick a football 70 yards. He's an amazing guy. Sure, I haven't ever gotten the chance ever to meet him, but I can already tell you that he's an amazing guy. He does nice things just because he's him and life's short. He inspired people like me without even knowing it. Blair doesn't even know who I am and here I am writing a chapter in my book about him. He's the reason that I stopped trying to impress my old friends. He's the reason I stopped trying to impress anyone but myself. I had confidence in myself. My self-esteem became higher, and I became happier. So, I wrote Blair a quick note thanking him for being him, and as a joke, I left my phone number on the bottom. From that day on, I can say, "I gave Blair Walsh my phone number!"

XXVI

The date was August 8th. I was sleeping really well because I was sick as can be. My whole body hurt. It started off as a sore throat and progressed into headaches then back and shoulder pain. Later, I began vomiting. My mom woke me up to tell me she was going to Spooner school to sign all of us up. This confused the hell out of me because the day before, she said that I could stay in Shell Lake. You're probably thinking, "Why in the world would you want to stay in a place that you hate?" Well, my problem was I cared about how people thought about me way too much. My old friends that drug me into depression, we don't have problems anymore. I've apologized. Although, I'm still waiting to hear an apology from them. I'm friends with them. Heck, the girl I called my best friend even wants to be close. I would honestly love so much to be friends with her again. She is such an amazing and funny person. The connection just isn't there anymore. We've tried talking, but it just isn't the same. I've lost hope for becoming best friends with her again. She was the best friend I ever had. Anyways, it's not like my old friends bully me or anything. We've gotten past that. We didn't have any issues this year. We were friends. For some reason, I wanted to be where I was before the beginning of seventh grade, friends with them. Probably because I was a teenager who wanted to be popular. Or was it because I wanted things to be as close to normal as they could be? Either way, it took me over half the year to stop worrying what my old friends thought of me. I stopped tagging along with them at lunch. I started putting myself around people who made me feel good about myself. People who appreciated my weirdness and humor. It was not an easy transition at all. It was a completely new start, and I didn't even realize that I was doing it. But I did, and I'm very happy about it. Guys, life is short. There is no time to be under appreciated. If you have "friends" that take advantage of you, or put you on a shelf until they need you, why are you friends? You cannot let people push you around. The sooner you realize it, the closer you are to happiness. You have power over who is in your life and who isn't. Make new friends. I know it isn't easy and you and your friends probably have so many good memories, but then again, how many bad ones are there? You don't have to be enemies with them, no. Slowly drift apart. Find people you have similar interests with. And if you have good friends that appreciate you, hold onto them and never let go. It's hard to find good people in the world we live in today. Don't take them for granted, go tell them thank you right now. It took me awhile to realize that if you aren't happy in a situation, you have the power to start over. It's your life. So, when I finally made new friends and stopped caring about my old friends' opinions, I got a little better. Scratch that, a lot better. I got rid of a big problem that I had. There was less stress and more laughs. Less tears and more smiles. That's something that made me want to stay in

Shell Lake. I don't care about others opinions so much anymore. I'm still working on it, but I've gotten so much better. It's all I lived for before; what people thought of me. I'm not going to let others thoughts on me, stop me from doing what I want. This is my life. I don't have to impress anyone. It's what I want. Honestly, everyone needs to let that sink in. THIS IS YOUR LIFE. If you don't like something and you have the power to change that, do it. You have to treat yourself. I mean, looking at how your actions will affect others is a great and caring trait to have, I am very glad that you have it. But sometimes, nice people forget that the life that they're living is for themselves. We need to be the best that we can be as an individual. Helping others is great

\- absolutely amazing. But helping yourself, beautiful, that's what you have to do first. Life will be so much less of a pain, if you make things easier on yourself.

XXVII

Death

I'm just now entering the terrible reality that my family isn't the same. It's now been a month after we've started moving into our new home in a different town. I don't know, it never really hit me. I knew that it would eventually. When someone would ask, "How are you feeling about your parents splitting up?" I said just that. "I don't know. It still hasn't hit me." And it didn't, but then, for the first time since my family was whole, I spent the night at my dad's house. At first, it wasn't bad. The first time it hit me was when I was sitting in my living room, typing. There was natural lighting coming in. I wasn't typing in the darkness like I did at my new house. It felt like home again. Heck, even the bathroom felt like home. It was just a satisfying feeling. I loved it and hated it at the same time. I mean, yeah, the feeling was absolutely amazing. I loved it, but I knew it wasn't going to last. When I woke up the next morning, it felt great. I got up, my dad made breakfast and I sat down to eat with my family. No, I sat down to eat with my Dad, brother, and sister. That's not my family; not all of it anyways. My mom wasn't there. So it's not home. The feeling was just so weird. I missed my family, but I couldn't tell anyone.

"Do you wish we still lived here?" I quietly asked my sister.

"Um… No, not really." She replied, not even paying attention to me.

Oh, I really can't tell anyone how I feel about this. No one feels the same. I can't tell my mom, that would be so selfish. I won't put my happiness in front of her wellbeing. They broke up for a reason and everything happens for a reason. So, whatever happens is supposed to I guess; even if it sucks. I felt alone, like I was in my own world. I wish I could describe the feeling. I was miles and miles away from being with my family, yet I was sitting right next to them. I am dead. I must be dead, right? The Earth really doesn't want me here. It seems to be doing everything in its power to make things go wrong. Why? It can be anywhere from my parents breaking up, to my mom spilling coffee on my shorts right before work. Life just seems to throw misfortunes in my path, all of the time. Should I take it as a sign of defeat, or try harder? It was 9:00pm. I just got done telling my dad about my plans for the future and he was impressed, as was I. My brother and sister were mad at me because I was laying in my sister's bed. My older sister's two sons were also at the house. I don't know exactly what happened. My boyfriend rarely takes me seriously when I talk suicidal. If I say something, he would say, "Babe, no, stop it." Aside from the fact that he doesn't use punctuation. But yeah, if I were to say, "Luke, I am going to kill myself in five minutes." He would say, "No babe, you don't have to." I mean, most people wouldn't know what to say. I don't expect anyone to be like, "Boom yes, I can talk anyone out of suicide!" No, it usually doesn't work that way.

But really, that's all that Luke would do. He doesn't take action at all; he thinks I am joking. So when I reached out to him for help, again, he didn't give any. My friend Seth, however, always takes action. So guys, for the third time, I had a plan for suicide. Well, as I have mentioned many, many times before, I think about killing myself a lot. I rarely take it into a lot of consideration or action. Only when it is really bad and I can't get a handle on my thought process. At the time, I was pretty sick. I had a buttload of pills from the doctor. You can probably see where my mind was leading me at this time. Now, I ignored the thoughts. I had the pills right next to me. Instead, I looked for a blade. I could take a knife, but my dad would see me. I was over two months clean at this point in time. I searched everywhere that I could think of, yet there was no sign of my slice of relief. The voices were getting louder and louder. My heart was beating so fast. Stop it. Stop this. I don't want to die. I really don't. I want to live. I have to live. I have a purpose and I know that. This isn't me. This isn't me. I felt like a psychopath talking to myself like this. It was odd to me. I kept throwing around positive words, and I kept trying to prove to myself that I am worth living. I am here for a reason. Why else would I be here, if I wasn't? I would not have been born. I wouldn't live, would I? But wait, am I really living? I've mentioned several times before that there's a difference between living and existing. I'm just existing. I am not creating fun memories. I am not going on fun road trips. I am not accomplishing anything. At that point in time, I didn't know that it's my fault I wasn't doing anything. If I want to be proud of myself, I need to set a goal and work to achieve it. This is my life. I am in control of it. I chose what I do with it. At that point of time, I didn't realize this. I let the voices control me. My mind was made up. I told Luke and Seth that I was serious. Luke came back with his usual response. I didn't want to hear it, so I left Luke on open. He didn't try to text me back or anything, he let me ignore him. Seth on the other hand, was freaking out. Seth was calling me and texting me like crazy. I went out in the kitchen, satisfied.

"Hey Ham, heading to bed?" My dad casually questioned.

"Yeah, I think so. I'm tired." I lied. Well no, I was going to go to sleep. Forever.

"Grab a water. Goodnight, I love you."

"That's actually what I was grabbing. Goodnight, I love you, too." I actually grabbed two. I wasn't sure what was going to happen, but I wanted to be prepared. Since it was a lazy day at home, I was all grubby. My hair was unbrushed and I was wearing zero makeup. I didn't have much of an option for clothes, so I put on my Mario pajamas and a comfy T-Shirt. Then, I walked into the bathroom and put on some cover-up and mascara, and brushed my hair. Hey, can't be super nasty looking when you're dead, right? So, I went back into my room all "dolled up" and sat down on a blanket on the floor. I looked around. Most of my belongings are either at my mom's or in the garbage. Even my bed. Ten missed calls from Seth. Great. There's nothing that he could say or do to change my mind. In that moment, I was gone. I really was. They took over. No texts from my boyfriend. Gee, I feel the love. With my mind made up, I dumped out all of the pills. Let's see what we have here. For starters, 3,000 MG of Zoloft - antidepressants - 6,000 MG of Ibuprofen, 900 MG of Claritin and 3,500 MG of Sulfa. All together, that was 13,500 MG of pills and I took 159 pills. I texted my boyfriend and friend and said the same thing, "Oh my god, I'm taking them." Seth flooded me with calls the whole time, but I kept ending them. Luke told me to throw them up and to stop. I took another handful of pills and then gagged and spit them out. Actually, only one came out. Do I actually want to die, because I am about to? I guess it isn't my choice anymore. I took the pills so I am most likely going to die. This is what I wanted, right? This is why I took them. To die. My dad is going to wake me up in the morning to tell me breakfast is done. It will actually be 12pm and he will tell me to get my lazy rear end up and out of bed. Then would come my chocolate lab, Maddie, running in to greet me. "Get 'er Maddie!" He would enthusiastically cheer. Maddie would sniff me, confused. What's wrong with my Ham? She's not breathing. Wake up! Wake up! I miss you already! She would lay her head down on me, and try to take in what's going on. You are my life. You're my best friend. Wake up, Camryn. I love you and I am hungry; it's chow time. My dad would start to worry. Why isn't she waking up? Why isn't she moving? Why is Maddie acting so strange? My dad, finally, would let the curiosity get the best of him. Slowly, he would walk over to his mini-him and pull the blankets off. My face is pale and emotionless. My dad wouldn't believe it. The day before, I was telling him about my future and plans, and he was so proud of me. He thought that everything was going to be alright again. My dad would shake me with tears rolling down his face. No, no. This isn't happening. Wake up! My dad would see my lifeless body and try to play back my voice. He would try so hard to remember me, but nothing would

come to mind. Nothing would resurface
because the pain of losing his
daughter, is so much. The hole in his
heart would be greater than most things
that he thought to be painful. He would
start to be able to push, and push, to
remember times together. I shouldn't
have been so mean. No, dad, you weren't
mean. You were raising me; you couldn't
have helped. There was a monster inside
of me greater than anything you could
ever imagine. Please don't blame
yourself. It's all my fault. No! Don't!
I wish that I could go back and tell
you what was going on, maybe you would
understand. I love you. I love you so
much. Why did you do this? Why couldn't
I help? What could I have done
differently? My dad would punch a wall
and feel like his whole world is
crumbling around him. He would be

speechless. My siblings and nephews would hear the loud bang and screaming, and come running to my dad's side.

"Dad! What's wrong? What happened?" The four children would keep demanding. My younger sister, Violet, would look at my pale, white skin and start screaming.

"No! No! Camryn! Wake up! This is all my fault!" Tears roll down her not-so-innocent face.

My sister would feel the most guilt that she would hopefully ever feel in her life. The same day that I killed myself, we were in a fight. My sister is a huge spoiled brat and I don't even remember what we were arguing about. Then, my sister kept saying, "At least I don't try to kill myself, Miss Suicide." She kept telling me that I deserved to die. I told her that I didn't, that I deserved to live, but she didn't listen. She always says stupid things that she doesn't mean when she's mad. But guys, you never, ever, tell anyone to kill themselves. No matter what you think, no one deserves to be told that. If someone is contemplating whether or not they want to live, you especially don't joke around and tell them to kill themselves. How would you feel if they went through with it? That's all it takes to push someone over the edge. Just a little push. You could even get charged with murder by telling someone to kill themselves, if they actually go through with it. My sister would carry that weight for the rest of her life. She told her sister to kill herself and she did. Some may say that that is dramatic. Honestly, though, if someone is on the fine line of deciding whether or not they want to continue life, then something that small, even if it's in a joking manner, can tip them off to their decision. Now, taking the pills wasn't because of my sister alone. No, there was a whole other world inside my head. I had the good, and the bad, and even worse. I'll put it this way, for someone perfectly healthy, buying a soda is a breeze. For people like me, it's seen as such a challenge. Easy tasks for you, seem like the impossible to us. But when we are pale and someone asks us if we are okay, we can't say anything but, "Yeah, I'm fine." because we are the only ones who see what's going on; who feel what's going on. I can't just tell people what's wrong in the gas station line. No, because most people won't understand and will think that it's just overreacting. That's what people don't understand. The little events just snowball, and snowball, until you have enough. It doesn't take something big to push someone. Honestly, it's probably just a bunch of little things piled up to bring them to this state of mind in the first place. Please, watch what you say. Please.

"Dad, this was my fault! She's dead because of me!" My sister would yell.

"Dad, what's going on? Why'd she say that Camryn is dead?" My little brother would pester and pester my dad to answer the question. Then, it hits him. He starts bawling his eyes out. His face turns almost as pale as mine.

"Camryn?" My baby brother would ask with little hope in his voice. My brother would just sit there and stare, bawling his eyes out. By this time, my dad would have already called 911. But my family is apart. Torn. Moments later, my dad would call my mom.

"Hi...." My dad's voice would say, drifting away.

"Hey, what's up?" My mom's last words before the terrible news hit her. The last news before she found out she lost her baby.

"Camryn... " My dad would start hyperventilating, and my mom would scream and demand answers.

She would already know that her daughter is dead. She would feel it in her gut; she would feel so lost and powerless. My mom was four hours away at this point in time, but she was on her way home. Once my mom would hear that I'm dead, she would put the pedal to the floor and never let off.

Mom! No! Violet and Ricky need you. Even dad needs you. Mom, please stay. Please, you have to. This family needs you. My mom would let the guilt of thinking that she wasn't a good enough mother control her. She would call herself a failure and next, my family would have to attend two funerals instead of just one.

Now, the paramedics would be hauling my lifeless body away. My brother, sister, and nephews would all be huddled together on my sister's bed; crying. Lost. My sister no longer had someone to give her advice on boys and my brother had no one to play Minecraft with. I will be gone.

Weeks later, my family is no better. I would think my death would only impact them for the first couple of days. Heck, in a year they'd even forget that I was gone. My little sister who loved to draw and write poems is still doing just that. Only she's drawing pretty pictures on her skin with a blade and the poems are her suicide letters. A week later, she hangs herself.

My innocent little brother who just sat and played video games, yeah, he smashed his Xbox the day I died. He is just bones; he doesn't even bother to eat anymore. He just sits in one spot in the dark all day long. Two weeks later, he is already dead before his heart even stops beating. Bones and a broken soul. He hasn't moved; his body lacks energy. He died of starvation and sleep deprivation. Just following the trend of people who loved and cared about me. Dying, he thinks, is the only way to escape the emotion and pain he is feeling. No, Ricky, you can get through this. You are so young, you have so much life in you. There are so many video games you haven't played.

My dogs, both of them stopped eating. They miss me and don't understand what's going on at all. They know that I was not happy. We tried to cheer her up. We would run around and lick her face and it worked! She was happy and we smelled it! But we don't smell her anymore. We miss her! Where is she? She knew the special spot behind our ears, she always called me a good girl and let me up on her bed when no one was around.

My boyfriend would cry. He wouldn't be the same. I wouldn't be there to support him or make him brush his teeth. If someone is your world, and you invest five months of your time into them, and then they suddenly go away, what do you feel? Empty. Your everything is gone and the emptiness from inside consumes you. My boyfriend would take his dark blue minivan and drive to my house. My boyfriend would look around, with every look he starts to remember every single memory. The driveway, I was always showing off on my little four-wheeler. The divots in the sand reminded him of my careless self, whipping donuts and popping wheelies, without a worry in the world. The garage, all of the chipmunk catching. We both tried so hard to try to catch the cute animals. The property was loaded with them when we first moved in, and we thought it would be cute to have a pet. We always spent so long looking for them in the wood pile, but every now and then, one would find its way into the garage. It was so much fun. The stove, that's where I made him his special bacon flavored spam and we seemed to have clicked better than usual. We laughed and he picked me up and spun me around. I was so happy. The bathroom, where he was forced to brush his teeth every time I noticed that he hadn't already. The stairs, where he carried me up and down for a couple of days because I ripped my toes open, no matter how many times I told him I was fine. The stairs, where we raced each other up and he always gave me a head start, but caught me and hugged me so tight I thought that he'd never let go. Happiness. The basement, oh, the movies we watched and the cuddling we did. I think we watched every single movie that I owned. My bunny cage, my little

Charlie was treated like my baby. Luke always told me that I treated it like it was my own kid. My bedroom. Wow, it still smells like me. My clothes were scattered around the floor, as usual. My bed was messy, and there were pop cans and water bottles disbanded around various places in the room. The funny videos we made, the adventures in the woods, the laughs. That, well, that was all gone. I pulled the rug out from under him and everyone else in my life. He sits and stares blankly wishing that he could turn back the clock; wishing that I was still there to tell him to have a good day or drive safe. He craved to hear the words that he was once so annoyed with. The random I love yous, the random thank yous that he took for granted, and never really thought anything of, will never come from my voice again. Never. I am dead and there's no amount of pain or guilt in this world that can bring me back. But, the amount of pain and guilt you feel, is enough to make you think that maybe life just isn't for you. So, my boyfriend lets it all consume him. He never returned home that day, most would think. But he, in fact, returned home. His home is in his girlfriend's arms, and that's just where he went. He missed me too much.

My friend, Seth, would completely shut down. He would sit and think about anything and everything under the sun. From things he could have done to maybe prevent this, to the times doing wheelies on four wheelers. I know for a fact that he would blame himself; he would think that everything is his fault. He would play back all of the times that he could have said something different. He would wish he had been more supportive and been able to say the right things. But, Seth is seriously my number one supporter. He really is. Seth is the first person that I would go to if I need advice, hands down. He has always jokingly called himself a therapist, but he pretty much was mine. He knew if I was sad, upset, or frustrated, and he would do everything in his power to help me. We mean a lot to each other. He's been there for me when no one else has been. I would have killed myself a long time ago, if I hadn't met Seth. He's convinced me that I have a purpose. He's the reason I am writing this book. Seth showed me that I am more than just a girl with a messed-up head. I have worth. I could never thank him enough for all that he has done for me. Then, I give up. I didn't even think about how he would feel. Inconsiderate. Seth says if I die, he wouldn't want to live either because he says that I am his world. No Seth, please don't do anything stupid.

My teachers at school would wonder if they were too hard on me, maybe they gave too much homework. They would sit and think about how in the world such a loud, energetic person could kill herself. I never showed any signs of killing myself. I mean, every day I put on the show of being so happy. Every single day I plastered the biggest smile on my face. So how would they know? Hmm, maybe when my choir teacher saw people teasing me for my self-harm scars, maybe that was something to act upon. Maybe when I came into class crying and put my head down every day for two weeks, something was wrong. Maybe when I turned in my paper talking about suicide, something was wrong. There were so many hints given. I wanted to be saved, but I didn't want to be upfront. I didn't want to literally say, help me please, I am going to kill myself. So, deep down, I hoped that they would pick up on those hints. I wanted it so bad. But they remained completely oblivious to the suicidal girl behind the smile. It fooled them because I was a professional on pretending and wearing my mask. I was a professional on giving the impression that I am the happy girl, who is really stupid, and isn't focused on school. Camryn… Camryn couldn't be suicidal. She is so happy. She makes everyone laugh. She's a great kid. She didn't really try in school, but she was always laughing. That's what they'll think. It will shock them. How could someone like me, kill themselves? My pain, it isn't visible to the people on the outside. I honestly don't tell anyone anything anymore. Everyone thinks that I am doing great. Everyone thinks that I'm the carefree blonde that loves making people laugh. My teachers probably never would have guessed that I was slowly but surely giving up. I wasn't just giving up in school, I was giving up one everything.

My best friend, Sidney, looks up to me. She is also suicidal. Sidney has tried to kill herself, but I try so hard to help her. I usually succeed most of the time, but I know how hard it is to say the right things to someone. If I ever talk suicidal, she says, "If you go, I go too." And sadly, she means it. She says that I'm the strongest person she knows and that I inspire her. If I showed her that I gave up, she wouldn't believe that she could keep going anymore either. So, when she would get a text from a friend saying that I was dead, she would scream at her phone and throw it on the ground.

"No! Camryn, no, please! This isn't real! Please, come over, I miss you so much!" My best friend would beg and scream up at the ceiling, wishing this was just a terrible, terrible dream.

"Camryn... Why? Why, why, why? Why did you give up? I love you so much... This, this isn't real."

Days later she would sit in her room and stare at the wall. She would go on her phone and look and all the photographs of us and videos of me being psycho. It would hurt so, so terribly. Sidney would reread all of our conversations. She would say that she should have been there for me. She would say that she should have taken me more seriously. Sidney always believed in me. It's not her fault at all. She helped me so much, and I could always talk to her. Eventually, she can't take it anymore. Nothing is worth it anymore it seems like. My best friend would miss me, and try to see me again. Another funeral to attend.

It was after thinking of things like this when I realized that I can't die. I actually do mean something to people. If I die, there would possibly be five deaths of my close friends and family members. Five people in this world have told me that if I killed myself, they wouldn't be far behind me. They love me. Oh my gosh, they love me. I can't die. But I am going to. I knew what I had to do. I picked up my phone and took a deep breath, this is what I need to do.

XXVIII

"Mom"

"Are you awake?"

"Please be awake."

"Mom"

"Mom"

"Mom, I tried to kill myself."

"I don't want to die."

My phone was getting blown up from Seth and Luke. Seth wouldn't stop calling me, and my boyfriend was Snapchatting me telling me to stop and to puke them up. I had been crying for a while already. After the last text, my mom replied.

"Answer your phone!!!"

I was confused because I hadn't received any calls or texts from her. So, I tried calling her. She answered, 250 miles away from me. The panic in her voice was so strong and urgent. I told her what I did, and she asked me to call Seth and stay on the phone with him, then she was going to call my dad.

"No!" I screamed.

"Babe, we need to get you to the hospital," she replied with sadness in her voice.

You're probably wondering why I didn't want my dad to know. Well, he is strict. I didn't know how he would react. I figured he would freak out. So, I called Seth.

"I don't want to die…" I said so quietly he could barely hear me.

"I know. Everything is going to be okay." I wasn't sure on how he was feeling about this.

"You have got to be kidding me!" My dad screamed from across the house.

"My dad is coming."

"Keep me on the phone."

"I'll try."

My dad storms in and keeps screaming at me. He takes my phone out of my hand and throws it.

"Get your shoes on, let's move it!" He hollered three inches from my face, "Get clothes, too, because you know where you're going after this."

He meant the hospital. The same hospital that I went months before for "help." No… I don't want to go back to that horrible place, and he knew that. There's a lot of guys who think that being scared or sad is something to be embarrassed by. It's not. It's great for guys to cry. It's great to express emotion; it is not something to hide from others. But, this society makes fun of guys when they aren't "tough" all of the time. When they cry, they're

238

labeled weak. When they're scared, they're labeled a wuss. That's not right at all. So, a lot of men think that they can't show emotion, so they act angry instead of being sympathetic. My dad has always been that way. My father was acting out in anger. I was getting screamed at left and right, and I just wanted my mom. I wanted to be with her more than anything. Of course, she was four hours away, and her car broke down the day before. So, she had no way to be with me. My dad wouldn't even let me talk to her. After he had thrown my phone, I picked it up and ran to the truck. I called my mom, but he kept yelling at me to end it. My dad isn't the type of person that you talk back to, but I did.

"I just want to talk to my fricken mom!"

He grabbed my phone out of my hands and put it next to him. My mom was scared, so she kept calling him but he kept hanging up, or he would answer and scream at her. I was crying the whole time, my siblings and nephews were all crying in the backseat of the truck, my dad just kept yelling at me and telling me what I did was stupid.

"You're kidding me." He would repeat and repeat.

It was probably about 11:00 pm now. Dark, rainy, and foggy. Suddenly, an ambulance goes by. It must be going to my house, but my dad didn't call 911. So, that part confused me. Maybe it's not going to my house then. All that I could do was cry, and listen to the disappointment in my father's voice. Was it worth it? Was it worth taking all of these pills? I feel like such a horrible person, but I was just doing what I thought to be right for me. But it's not what's right for others. As we arrived at the hospital, I felt so nervous. I didn't know what to expect, I mean, people never talk about these things. I've heard people mention getting your stomach pumped, and I had no idea how that even worked in the first place. So, the lady at the reception remained perfectly calm, she took her time and wasn't really shocked. I live in a small town; I hope things like this don't happen so often that they act like it's no big deal. I don't think that they do because again, no, "please don't kill yourself. How are you feeling? What's on your mind?" I was then led into a tiny room and asked questions. After I had told the nurse what I took, she got scared. She invited me to follow her, and we went into an emergency room right by the entrance. Alright, they are going to help me. I had to take off my shirt, and they put several wires all around my body, it was a new experience for me. Then I was getting blood drawn, time after time, again. Doctors always have trouble getting blood from me. I have super small veins, so it took several pokes to find the right spot and several minutes to get the blood out, finally. Then the next hand was getting drawn, too. The nurse did something wrong, so the blood went all over, just as my brother and sister were walking in to see me. They had both been crying. My sister walks in and sits down.

"I'm dying." She complains,

My brother and I just look at each other funnily.

"Really, you're dying?" He said to my ignorant sister.

Then he and I laughed while my blood shot all over the floor. A cop came in to see me, so my family had to leave. The officer and I had the type of conversation you would expect. I was asked a bunch of questions like, "Why did you do this? Are you abused? Do you do drugs?" And blah blah that he's required to ask everyone. I waited in the room alone, for hours. Alone. I was alone. No nurse to talk to, no family, friends, am I even important? I felt useless. Then the cop came back in to put me on the line with The National Suicide Prevention Lifeline. Gosh, don't even get me started on that. Well, I am all riled up now so might as well get started on it. So, the first time that I went to the hospital, I gave you a tiny bit of information about what went on. Yes, they asked questions like the cop did. Not anything about how I was doing emotionally, ones that only benefit them. Their intentions are good; I just don't understand why they think that they're helpful. I'm very happy that there's an organization with the right idea, they just don't do the proper procedures. After I had gotten out of the hospital the first time, I was given a sheet with the number of the hotline. I wasn't crazy about it since I just saw how it worked, but I tucked it away just in case I needed it again. So, one day, I am alone, and I thought that it seemed like it was a good day to kill myself. I wasn't on my pills then either, so I didn't have the right mindset. I walked to a park and waited for the train to go by. But wait, maybe there's a better solution. So, I took out my phone and called the number. First, there's stupid fancy music playing for a while; then you are directed to an automatic voice recording of some lady talking super slow. She babbles on about how they are going to help and how much they help the Veterans. Not to mention the fact that they have to take the time to repeat everything in different languages. Then you get to pick a number, after waiting through all of that, again, you're put on hold. Great. Leave a person with a gun to their head on hold. So smart. You get put with someone nearby, and they don't say anything relevant. They just offer places for help. That angers me. But I've tried it several times since then, hoping that it maybe would be different. It never is, it's always the same old thing. Disappointment. No help, why? I mean, I am so glad that they do something, in an attempt at least, but what they try isn't effective. It must be hard to try and balance everything that is going on. It must be hard to try to get everyone on with someone so fast and have one on one time. Well, guess what, this is important. We need to make this bigger. We need to have more operators and professionals in to help. Depression and suicide are rising, and the help we need is decreasing. Let's do something about that.

So, I was asked a bunch of stupid questions and whatnot. Never a, "Hey, how are you doing?" Just, "Are you abused?" Which is important, but go with the situation and the person at hand first guys, come on. It was the same second time around than the first. There was help all around, but I wasn't getting any. Most of them probably don't really know what's going on. Yeah, they're trained professionals, but most of them probably never went through this. The books they give you in college can tell you what depression and suicidal thoughts are, but they don't give you situations. The books, they don't put you in the shoes of the writer, and most people fail to connect unless they have to work around this in their everyday lives. That's why I am writing this; I am hoping to give you a taste of what this is. Not all of the blah blah education that really doesn't seem to leave the same impression on you. The people that I've worked with, I've had only two whom I think know what they're talking about. What they say actually helps. Otherwise, everyone goes by the books, but the books are wrong. Well, not necessarily wrong. Just not right. That's not how you should pass information onto a person. You have to put them in your shoes so they understand. The books, they give you a pretty good idea of the symptoms. The thing is, everyone has sad days, and everyone has days they think of suicide. So, people will research this on their own because they don't learn it in school, and they're curious. People will then self - diagnose themselves with depression. Guys, it's not something to be proud of. I am not saying that you need to be embarrassed if you actually have depression, but if you think it's cool to pretend you have it for sympathy, screw you. Depression isn't just being sad. No, there is so much more to depression, and I am showing you by writing my story. Depression is not fun. Depression is not something to go show off to your friends so that they feel bad for you. Depression has a mind of its own and it makes hard times even harder. Depression isn't something that you can ignore, it changes your life. Just because you're lazy, you can't just blame it on depression. It angers me so much to hear about people thinking this is okay, they think it's an excuse not to try. Honestly, it's a reason to try harder. Get through this. Fight hard, I know you can. You can show everyone that depression, well, you can work with it. You can show the world what you are capable of. Eventually, people will know how to help. Until then, we have to keep fighting. We have to keep fighting to stay alive, make a difference and show the world what we can do.

XXIX

After endless visits from strangers, stupid questions, and lots of tears, I fell asleep. I can't wait to wake up and see my mom. I need her so much. I really need my boyfriend too. I have to have him next to me. My friend, Seth, would be there too, happy to see that I was alive. I can't wait to see everyone. I need comfort right now. I haven't heard anyone tell me that they were happy that I was alive or anything, and I was in need of it very badly. I craved to hear the words of reassurance. I needed to know that reaching out for help was right. I needed to know that I was loved. The last time I remember looking at the clock, it was around 1:00 in the morning. My heartbeat wasn't on track, so they had to keep me overnight. My dad went home, so I was left alone until falling asleep. I had so many different wires hooked up to me it was unbelievable. I had different medications being put into my body with tubes. I fell asleep to the sound of beeping, and the ticking of the clock. Hmm, is life really for me? When the bad thoughts flowed through my head again, I would just remember that soon my mom would arrive. She should be there at two, right? I couldn't wait. My boyfriend, I wonder why it's taking him so long. Maybe he was just planning on going in the morning. Oh boy, seeing someone special to me would help so much. I can't even describe to you how much I wanted someone to be at my side. I couldn't wait. I wanted to know that

living was the right choice. I wanted
to feel loved.

XXX

It was four o'clock in the morning; then I felt a nurse tugging on my wires. Yay, my people will be here. My crusty eyes look up in a hurry, but soon my body is filled with disappointment instead of relief. No one was there. Just a nurse trying to put me in a wheelchair. No one was there. I was alone. Hmm, maybe they would show up later. I looked at the clock; it was only 4:00 in the morning. My dreary eyes looked around as the nurse pushed me through the dark hallways and passed the heavy set doors. Eventually, I was led out of the emergency room and into an actual hospital room. I was forced to use the bathroom, then put right back into bed. I laid down, boy, was I exhausted.

Sleep sounded perfect but it seemed almost impossible to sleep with all of the wires and needles stuck into me. Until I tried to fall asleep, then it was easier than I expected. I woke up again at 8:00 am. My eyes had the weight of the world on them. It sounded like there were people in the room. Yes, my mom and dad and boyfriend made it. I have company. I couldn't begin to explain to you how excited I was to be connected with reality once again. To feel alive, to feel my worth once again. Finally. My hope filled eyes looked up to see my wonderful family. Only, they were not there. I was informed that my heart stopped working while I was at the hospital. I was so close to being gone forever, and there was no one by my side. I died, and if I wasn't saved, it would have been alone.

Let me tell you something that is 100% truth. I, Camryn Nasman, would have rather died and not been revived, then to have woken up with no one by my side. Does anyone even care about me? No one was there. No one. I woke up, and no one was there to show me that he or she cared about me and loved me. That's when I started repeating in my head, "I wish that I was dead. I wish that I was dead." And I did. I wished that I was dead. The pain of waking up alone just threw me down. It is worse than falling off the top of the highest building because at least you don't suffer. At least you don't stay awake at night, unable to convince yourself you are loved. You no longer believe you mean anything to people. I must have just been overreacting. I must have wanted to believe people would care if I died. The truth is, I was in a situation to die and nobody showed that they cared. Nobody showed that I was worth their time. Please, someone, take me out now. Take all of the life-saving gadgets off of me, I don't want to live. I don't want to fight. Please, someone, help me. If you want what's best for me, kill me. I am not loved. I am not special. No one wants me here, please. I still hadn't heard anyone say any word of encouragement. No one sat down to talk to me about how life was, how I was doing, or what I was feeling. Nobody wanted feedback from me. All of the information that was asked was for them. They have to; it's their job. Everything that was asked by the cop and social workers was for work. Nothing personal, nothing about my own well being. Just so they don't lose their job. Just so they keep getting paychecks. Getting the suicidal patient stable emotions, that's part of the job, right? You have that job because you like helping people, so help. Go above and beyond what the law says. Make sure the person is going to be alright. Having someone to talk to is so important in a time like this. I had no one. Left alone. Have someone- anyone - come and have a personal conversation. Come on guys, let's change this. We need to help the patients. We need to make them feel like there's someone there for them, and I know that you want to help. You just don't know how. I know that most people would be willing to sit down and have a normal conversation with someone in need of it. Don't start off with heavy-duty topics. Ask them how they are doing, what school they go to, their dreams, blah blah. Then get into the heavy topics. Just let the conversation feel natural, let it flow nicely. You don't want the person to feel overwhelmed or used. They want to feel like you actually have an interest in their future. Show them that what they have to say, matters, because it does. It matters so much, but there are so many shitty people in this world, they feel like they don't matter. Prove them wrong, make them feel special. That's what the job is about. Helping people. How beautiful is that? You not only save their physical life, but you save or help their emotional and mental life as well. In my opinion, that's the best thing ever. You are such a hero. Thank you for everything that you do. Thank you for making a difference.

XXXI

Who reading this is happy all of the time? Who reading this, never, ever thinks about suicide or how their death would affect others? Who in here is always motivated to do everything? Who reading this has amazing self-confidence? Huh, no one? Wow! You must have depression! I mean, those are the symptoms, right? So, you must have depression. Now, go tell all of your friends and upload a few sad quotes onto your Instagram. Use your "mental health" as an excuse not to try. Use it for sympathy. Go on, self-diagnose yourself. Make life easier. Guys, this isn't right. So, a complaint of mine had been that schools don't teach about mental health. I just started my freshman year a couple weeks ago.

Health is one of my classes, and we did, in fact, start learning about depression. At first, I was super excited, until we got into it. It really ticked me off. The slideshows and presentations that we watched, well, they made depression sound like a choice. It was kind of like, "You have to be nice to yourself; otherwise you'll get depression." Which loving yourself doesn't always help with a chemical imbalance in your brain, does it? We were handed these worksheets on wellness. We had to take a test, and it was about loving yourself and taking care of yourself. It told you how screwed up you were if you weren't perfect. In other words, it made everyone in the class feel like shit. If you aren't happy all of the time or don't think you're perfect, your life will suck. Life isn't all good guys. If someone tries to make you feel bad for your feelings, just zone them out. It's life; nobody said that it was easy.

XXXII

You've heard about Luke. Heck, you've heard A LOT about Luke. You know how much I love and care for him. I would do anything and everything under the sun for him. He's my world; the reason I smile. Well, we are going to go back to the date of September 7th. Luke's birthday is on Friday. What should I get him? What should I plan? It has to be as special as him, he deserves it. My world deserves the world in return, so I should try and give it to him.

I asked my mom what we could do, and we had my little cousin Rylee's birthday that day at the park, too. There would be a photo booth and stuff, so I thought that kind of sounded like fun. Luke has a family party on

Saturday, and I was invited via Facebook. The whole thing was all about drinking, which I wasn't very crazy about. I asked my mom if I could go, but she said she didn't want me to be around drunks. I didn't mind at all, because I didn't want to be around drunks either. My mom just said to Luke, "Why don't you just stay here? We can throw a little party here. Put up the projector, rent some movies and you can invite some friends." Disappointment filled his face. He wanted to drink on his birthday, and nothing would change that. I mean, no, I am not crazy about thinking of his drinking, but it's his 18th birthday. So, I was okay with it for the most part.

Thursday, he was supposed to come over and hang out. With no texts from him, I waited. I never saw any sign of him, though. Not one. If you aren't going to show up, at least tell me that. At least give me a heads up, so I don't get filled with more disappointment. But no. He never even texted me. Alright, don't get mad. He wouldn't blow you off on purpose; something must have come up. He is simply just busy; you will have an explanation later. I told myself these things. After hours, he finally Snapchats me, "Hi babe." I didn't freak out on him and ask him where he was; I had a normal conversation with him. After a while, I asked him where he was, not aggressively, and he said going to Duluth. Well, what the heck? Maybe he just forgot. Maybe he just doesn't care. I'm not important. No. He loves me very much; I am very important to him. He didn't give me an explanation of why he went there. I asked him if he wanted to go to my cousin Rylee's birthday party, then go to the movies and out to eat. My boyfriend said that he would love that. So, I made reservations and planned out our amazing day. I figured he would come over later. He stopped talking to me not long after he started, and I didn't hear from him until way, way later. I stayed up late so that I could wish him a happy birthday. He never showed up, so I just made a cute video to post on Instagram. I bought him a card earlier, so I wrote a whole bunch of lovey dovey stuff in it. After waiting and waiting, I ended up falling asleep at 11:52 pm and didn't get to say happy birthday.

Right away on Friday morning, I said happy birthday to my handsome man, and he didn't open it for awhile. Around 7 am, I knew something was up. He was supposed to be up and ready for school. Finally, he informs me that he has a funeral. I felt terrible for him. He had to go to his uncle's funeral on his birthday. I was then more determined to make his day better. I wrote a bunch of notes that I was going to put in his locker after each class, and I was planning on having the secretary give him a birthday shoutout. Those two plans were off the table since he wouldn't be at school until the end of the day, but afterwards, we would have a great time. The day went very slowly. I missed him. I wanted to be with him on his special day. I really did. You get to see him later.

That's something to look forward to, right? After a while, I texted Luke, but something was different. The change in communication. The change in the way he was wording things; so simple. He had done this right before he broke up with me a couple weeks ago. No, don't think like that. He promised that he wouldn't leave you again. He promised that you mean so much to him. You believe him; you trust him. You are his world; he won't leave you. Calm down.

Luke told me he wouldn't be back until later. I told him we would have to leave at five, and he said that he should be back by then. Alright, good. I still get to have a fun afternoon with him. After school, I started to get worried. Luke never showed that he was excited to hang out; he never showed any emotions. He doesn't like me. Why do I care so much? Why do I expect him to give back everything that I give? No. He loves me. He is just sad, he had a funeral to go to. Help him get through this and don't take it personally.

Right before five, Luke said he was not going to show up. Oh. I go to Rylee's party, waiting for a text from my boyfriend. Waiting for him to say, "Just kidding babe! Be there soon, I love you." I craved to hear the words that would never come. I thought yelling at him would be overreacting. It's his birthday, too. So, I didn't nag much, even though I was super, super upset about it.

Hours later, my friend Sidney texts me and asks me to go to the Webster football game. Luke probably wouldn't want me to go. There is likely to be a lot of guys there. I have to respect Luke's decision. Right? Well, I did have a whole night planned for us, and he completely blew me off, didn't he? Hmm, maybe I should go. I have nothing going on and I miss Sidney. I texted Luke and told him that I was going to the game. He didn't ask me not to go. Although, I think he got mad about it. So, around 7:15 pm I got there. I got to see a whole bunch of friends, and it was great. I thought about Luke the entire time. Being around all of these guys didn't make me fall for them. I just noticed how lucky I was to have Luke. It just made me more thankful to have him; I want him. I'm so glad that he is mine. I didn't flirt with any guys; I barely even talked to any. I didn't need to. I mean, I already have the most amazing guy in the world.

Afterwards, Luke was being weird. We never said I love you, goodnight or anything romantic. I had the odd feeling that he was going to break up with me. It was the same vibe that I felt before. I felt disconnected from him. We were still dating, but I felt alone. I felt like he was gone and I couldn't lose him. My god, I couldn't lose him. He is my everything. He is my will to live. He gives me the motivation to be the best that I can be.

I know that I'm young, I really do, but, I honestly believed that he was the man that I was going to marry. I could see my future so clearly now, but it was only if it involved him. My heart hurts so bad. He is totally ignoring me. Luke is going to leave. He can't, he can't leave. I love him. I love him so much. Please, please. I need him.

I didn't know what to do. It would be different if I wasn't at a friend's house, but I am. I can't cry. The reason behind that isn't because Sidney wouldn't let me or help me; she would. Sidney would do anything to help me. Anything. She wouldn't see me as weak; she would boost me up. But the thing is, I can't cry in front of people. It's so weird. I can be on the verge of tears, but won't shed a single one if there're people in front of me. But as soon as I turn the corner, it all falls down so hard. I can hold it all in until I'm alone. That's where I can cry. That's where I can think and try to come up with a solution.

That's what I needed to do; be alone. I waited. I wanted to cry so bad. Finally, Sidney fell asleep. I just laid on the floor, staring off at nothing. All that I could see is empty nothingness, and ironically, it's all that I could feel. Luke, I need you. You have to stay. I felt like someone with scissors came up and snipped the last bit of connection we shared. Luckily, they missed the hope that I still had. If Luke meant everything that he said, he wouldn't want to leave. He would want to make this work, no matter how hard things get. After hours of wondering what I did wrong, I fell asleep.

The next morning Luke was the first thing on my mind. Nothing new. Only this time, instead of being followed with a smile, it was followed with a blanket of godawful thoughts and a negative view of myself. After a while, my mom arrives to bring me home. That's where it all goes down.

Luke's 18 now. I'm 14 and turning 15 soon. Technically, it isn't illegal to date. However, sexual contact… that, that is illegal. So, Luke texted me and told me that we couldn't be together. He said that he was scared. If someone accused us of having sex, he would be charged with statutory rape. I think it's stupid. We can wait. If he loves me, we can wait. This can't be all that he wants. It can't. He loves me for me, right? Oh god. Does he love me for me? Is he just using me because I seem easy? My thoughts were eating me alive.

XXXIII

The pain wasn't any less the second time around. Luke left me. He gave up again. I believed everything he said. I actually thought that he regretted losing me and never would want to again. Why did I believe him? Why? I should've known he was going to hurt me again. I'm never good enough. I love him so much. What am I going to do now? I didn't know. I didn't know what to do. I tried so hard not to cry. Great. More staying up until 6am. More sleepless nights because I always dreamt of his cute face coming back for me. Every night, I dreamt that he returned. He was in my arms and mine all over again.

When I woke up… Oh gosh, when I woke up, the pain stung my whole body.

Luke's gone. My everything, my life, isn't even mine anymore. All that I could do was miss him. I missed him so much. Goodbye good self-esteem, goodbye smiles, goodbye love, goodbye motivation, goodbye laughs, goodbye me. I wanted to die, because hello tears, hello sleep deprivation, hello confusion, hello trust issues, hello low self-esteem, hello worthlessness. Everything is going to get bad again. Everything will be like it was before I met him. And guys, that's not okay. That's not okay at all.

I've invested everything that I had into him. I told myself that I need him when really, all you need is yourself. Never, ever let your happiness depend on another person. You never know when they'll leave. You never know when it'll all get taken from you. You need to know how to make yourself happy. You need to be kind to yourself. You need to be your own motivation, you need to be your own happiness, you need to be your own number one supporter, you need to be you. You need to be everything you need. You always have yourself, everyone else, well, they can leave you at any given moment. You need to be able to be successful with just yourself. You cannot let it depend on someone else. Sure, it's great to have people in your life, but that's actually just a bonus. If you think about it, it is so important to be able to love and believe in yourself... So important. You need to be able to do all of the things that you depend on others to do, really, you do. Because what are you going to do when they're gone? You have to be able to do things on your own. You have to love yourself.

Realizing this, I made a bunch of plans to do new things. I had the crazy idea of starting to public speak. It would be a challenge, but speaking at schools would be something right up my alley. I would love to do that. Helping people, wow. That would be amazing. That's all that I want to do is help people. I really do. It fills me with purpose. I feel like I'm worth something when I help someone, I'm here for a reason, right? I mean look, I just made a positive difference in that person's life. Honestly, for me, there's no greater feeling.

I am dedicating my whole life to helping people now. It's what I see in my future; it's so clear. Along with that was Luke… He was my future. I was myself being successful with him. But I didn't have him anymore. So, I worked my butt off to be happy and successful without him. It paid off. Sure, everytime that I was alone, I thought of Luke and all of our memories.

After a few days, I convinced myself that I was better off without him, not fully, but it helped a little bit at least. I missed him so much, but I wouldn't let myself believe it. I tried so hard not to love him, but, it's not my choice, is it? You can't choose if you love someone. You either do or don't, no forcing feelings, it doesn't work that way.

I tried so, so, so, hard just to get him off my mind. I constantly had to be talking to someone. Whether it was making jokes in class to the person sitting next to me or skyping my friend

Seth until I fell asleep, I always had to try and distract myself. It worked fine. Fake it until you make it I guess… I'd like to say that I just got over Luke, but I didn't. All that I could think of was him. I wondered how he was doing without me, if he misses me, how his day was, if his favorite drink was still Pepsi. God, everything reminded me of him, every single damn thing reminded me of his cute self. I mean everything. He was always on my mind, and I wish that I was on his. I missed him so much.

XXXIV

It was a week since we broke up. It wasn't long, but it felt like years. One of my really good friends, Jordan, came over and brought me chicken nuggets. He always cheers me up. I had a really great time with him. I've been friends with him for a while. I met him at state ice fishing, along with Luke and John. So, I ate the chicken nuggets, and we sat down to talk. We were always laughing when we were together. It felt great to have company, and Jordan makes me laugh more than most people. My tummy hurt from laughing so hard. We both have the same type of humor, and we are both really weird. We watched a few funny videos and looked at pictures on Facebook and laughed our butts off. I needed that a lot. See, I can laugh without Luke. Sure, it still hurts and I still love him to death, but I will survive this.

After laughing and making jokes, we sang karaoke. It was really fun. There were jokes being thrown left and right along with our singing. My mom joined in. I had a blast. Then, Jordan brought up Luke. No, no, I survived the night this far… Hopefully, I can keep going. I was distracted most of the time that he was over, but I was still thinking of Luke on occasion.

I saw a picture of Luke on one of my friend's stories on Snapchat. Her name was Heidi. He was at her house on his phone. The first thing I thought to myself was, "Awe, he's so cute." He's good friends with the girl's brother, that's why he was there. I missed him alot, but carried on. The girl texted me and so I texted her back. We sent random faces to each other. We used to be super good friends and we both always make funny faces.

She sent a picture of Luke and asked if I still liked him. I really didn't know what to say. I love him, oh god, I love him to death. But, we aren't right for each other. We can't be, right? Oh well. I just responded with, "That's classified information. (;" She then said that I seemed happier without him.

That part was true. I did look way happier, but that's because I was trying so hard to be happy and to look happy. I was talking to new people and trying new things, I was becoming happy. Not necessarily happier without him, just happier with trying new things. I felt like myself again. So, I just said, "Oh" and she asked if I was. I said, "God, no I'm not." I hoped that she wouldn't tell him, but I figured that she would. Then I knew that she did. She said, "What would you do if this faggot texted you." I simply said, "Text him back." because it's true.

During all of this, I was confused, but happy. Jordan was filling me in on a bunch of shit that I would never have expected from Luke. It made me sad. He said that this summer, he saw Luke come in with three different girls. Gosh, that hurt. He said that Luke banged like seven girls in middle school. It really angered me, only because he told me completely different before. There was just a lot of crap that made me upset.

It kind of made me feel better, in a way. Well, I can do better than a liar and a cheater, right? That made me feel better. However, a big chunk of me didn't believe what Jordan was telling me. I don't think Luke would lie to me, and then cheat on me, would he? But then again, maybe he would. He never really told me anything. I always asked how his day was and stuff, but he never went into detail about what he did. I rarely knew where he was. I sure hope he wouldn't. I loved and cared about him a lot. Life just sucks butt sometimes.

XXXV

After days of pretending to be happy at school, endless nights of no sleep, fake smiles, and awkward glances, that night, I got a text from him. My heart raced, and I felt like crying. Should I open it? Should I respond? I paced back and forth. After countless arguments with myself, I decided to open the first text that I got from him since we broke up.

"I'm sorry."

Are you serious? Gr. Yep, that makes my aching heart feel so much better for sure. I was getting angry. Was he trying to make everything less awkward and be friends, or get back together?

"It's okay." I responded, even though it really wasn't.

"No, it's not."

I don't remember exactly how our conversation went. He told me about how much he missed me, and later asked to hangout. Let's just say I cried and felt differently than I felt before.

The next day I folded clothes so that I could go see him. I didn't dress fancy or anything, just joggers and a t-shirt. I didn't know where we were going so I didn't dress very nicely. Chances are, we aren't going anywhere where I'd need to dress up, so I didn't. At 1:00, he arrived at my house. I was very nervous. I walked over to his car and sat down. I said, hi, and looked out the window. And with that, we drove off. Hmm, I wonder how long this car ride will be? I wonder if it'll be awkward the whole time. The ride was not long at all. We drove to a boat landing not far from my house. Oh no, is he going to murder me or something? Why in the hell would he bring me to a boat landing? It looked beautiful, though. Nature almost always relaxes me. Maybe that's why he brought me here. We stepped out of his car and walked over to the glistening water. Gorgeous. I looked down at my feet to see what kind of beautiful stones I could find. Luke was already ahead of me. Before I knew it, he was hugging me. It felt weird and I struggled to break free. Next thing I know, we are face-to-face and I'm looking into his amazing blue eyes. He leans in for a kiss. I didn't want to kiss, but I didn't fight it. We then hugged and skipped rocks and talked about life. Luke picks me up and sets me on top of his car.

"I have cancer." he said with his face stone cold.

I couldn't believe it. I started to cry. At first, I thought he was joking, but who would joke about something like that?

"Really?" Please tell me this isn't real.

A smile comes across his face and I twisted his nipple really hard. I was really mad that he would even joke about something like that, but relieved at the same time. He's sick for doing that.

After that, we drove to one of the most beautiful places that I had ever seen in my life. It was bear hunting season, so we had to be careful. We walked down these gorgeous steps taken over by weeds and moss. There were giant vines over us. It felt like a kingdom. It was beautiful. We approached a stream. It looked so pretty. There was a mini waterfall too. It was just simply breathtaking.

Next, he took me down this path. There were swamps all over, but they looked gorgeous. Weeping willows swayed above us. I felt like I was in a fairy tale. Then I tripped over a tree root and I was living my life once again. Luke picked me up and walked me down a hill. I felt like a princess.

After discovering some beautiful places, I told him that I had to be back home. I texted my mom and told her that I was on my way home. We got back and sat on the porch. I was confused. Are we dating? No, he never asked me out. Would you take him back? We took some selfies with the Snapchat filters and laughed. Then, he said the words I prayed for the week before seeped out of his mouth.

"Will you go out with me?" Luke said with a smile.

"No." I replied, mimicking his cute smile.

"What?" He was so shocked and confused.

I laughed and said, "Let me think about it."

XXXVI

We cuddled on the couch and just talked about stuff. We were talking about something, I don't remember exactly what, and I jokingly asked, "How many girls did you have sex with this weekend?"

"Just one." He responded, casually.

"Wait, what? With who?"

It turns out, he had sex with a 24 year old. No... are you kidding me? The girl's name is Holly, and she is fricken 24 years old. I was furious. I knew about her. She is Luke's cousin's best friend. He talked to her all the time while we got back together, but I thought that it was different stuff, not planning to have sex.

She had sex with my boyfriend. I went completely crazy on the inside. But on the outside, I stood up, put on my shoes and walked out the door. Once I was outside, I ran to beat hell. There's no way I am going to be the second choice.

I sat down behind a giant tin tub in the woods and cried. Keep in mind it's pitch dark out now. The voices crept up behind me and repeated how stupid and worthless I was. *He left you for her. He never loved you. No one loves you. How could anyone love you?* Wow... I wasn't his first pick. I was second. I felt like crap. I wasn't wanted or loved by the person I wanted more than anything. After a couple minutes of sitting in the dark alone, I hear Luke's voice. Gross. I wanted nothing to do with him. I wanted him

out of my life forever. Luke runs
around frantically trying to find me,
but gives up and goes inside.

XXXVII

It's Monday, September 19th. Today is the worst day that I've had in awhile. I am currently typing, but I am supposed to be doing homework, and I have a feeling someone is watching my computer. Oh well.

Yep, just got yelled at for writing for the first time this school year. Dumb. Well, this chapter will start off with a flashback, here we go. So, the day started off decent. I was riding in the car with Luke and I kept getting reminded of him banging another chick. It hurts, it really does. It's more the intimate part of it than anything. Him kissing her, like he kissed me… It hurts. It hurts so bad. So, I wasn't in the best mood. I always get so sad when I think of that situation.

Not one person tells me that giving him one last chance is the smart choice. So, is it? I mean, I like him a lot. You as the reader know this. You know how much he means to me. But I don't know if I can get over this. Sure, we weren't dating, but he got over me so fast. All of his attention was on another girl. I wasn't loved. I wasn't first. He picked someone else. It really hurts to think of it. Luke would always be my first choice. Always. I couldn't even imagine being with someone else. Seriously, if I could have anyone it'd be him. I'm so lucky to be able to have the person that I want… I really am. But, he didn't want me. He wanted her. I keep trying so hard to get over it but I can't.

He swears he will never leave me again, but I already had terrible trust issues, and now I have this. It changed everything. The people I thought that I trusted, I no longer trust just because I believed everything that came out of my boyfriend's mouth. I never second guessed or questioned his words. I believed that, wow, there actually can be someone who loves me. I believed that it was possible for someone like me to be loved by an amazing person, I believed that maybe, I got lucky this time. Maybe life isn't a total bitch all of the time. I'm blessed with an amazing man in my life. I couldn't ask for anyone else. I believed there was something to make life so much more bearable.

I had a bonus, but I didn't think of him as a bonus. I bought into the Disney movies that claim everyone has happy endings and Prince Charming will come and save you. That's not how it is at all, but that's what most humans believe. They see the "happily ever afters" but, guess what guys? Life isn't some fairy tale. Life is so hard, and we are all going to have rough times. Don't give up. I know it's so hard, but you can't give up.

You don't realize it in the moment, but you learn so much from the good and bad experiences. It's beautiful in the end. You are alive. Even last year when you never thought that you'd make it, here you are now. Alive, breathing, living. I'm so proud of you. And next year, when something even worse comes up, you won't think that you can make it but beautiful, you can. I know that you can.

As you know, I dislike school with a burning passion. I went on this particular Monday in a decent mood, I said until I started thinking about Luke with that girl, then it got bad. I didn't really talk to Luke in the morning. Instead of us hanging all over each other, we acted as if we didn't see each other. Note, that this was our first day at school dating since we broke up.

First period I have Physical Science. How exciting. So, the girl that I was sitting next to was a friend of mine and Luke's. She told me a whole bunch of stuff that hurt, but I was glad to hear it. I could feel my body tightening. I really wanted to punch something, but I couldn't. I was at school in the middle of a lecture. My face started to feel hot and my throat felt swollen. No, now is not a good time. Deep breaths, deep breaths.

Finally, I had enough. I punched the table and walked out of the classroom. Then came the hyperventilating. No, not now. Come on, please stop. It's fine. It's fine. Wait, no. It's not fine. It hurts. Following those words, I banged my head continuously against the wall. Why am I never good enough? I tried so hard to keep him happy, I tried so hard to be enough for him. I guess I'm nothing to him. The tears of failure rolled down my face, I couldn't breathe. After a while, one lady teacher came to see me. I didn't want to talk to her. She wanted to bring me to talk to someone, but I really just needed a couple minutes alone, and I'd be fine again and ready for class. This isn't just some strange phenomena for me. I usually know when it's going to happen, and I'm learning my triggers. She won't let me have my space. After arguing and pointless conversation, she put me in a room filled with several people. Great. I really couldn't take it. So, I walked out. The lady one room over saw me walk out, and tried to follow me. Umm no. Leave me alone. I got halfway down the Jr. High hallway and the guidance counselor called my name from the entrance. I looked at her and continued walking. Can't these people tell that I just want to be left alone? I guess not. She continued to call my name. I love and respect my guidance counselor very much, but I just wanted to be left alone. Finally, I turned around and let her catch up with me.

"Can I just walk?" I asked calmly.

"Of course. Walk first, then we'll talk." She responded, understanding my request.

So, we walked one lap around the hallways and she leads me into her office. I explained to her why I was upset. I told her about Luke. Luckily, she always says the right things. How she responded made me feel a lot better. Now, I told you that not one single person told me that I was doing the right thing. However, I was still doing what I wanted, regardless of everyone else's opinions. She told me that giving him another chance wasn't stupid. I felt a lot of weight come off of my shoulders.

After a couple minutes of talking, I went back to class. It was fine being there. I felt way better. So, I continued on until the bell rang for the second period. Usually, Luke meets me coming out of science, but he didn't. Considering what I just heard, I was scared. Why didn't he greet me? Is he mad at me? Did I do something wrong? I don't know what I did. I mess everything up. We walked past each other without even talking. He must be mad at me.

I set my stuff in the health room and took a couple laps around the halls. Eventually, the thoughts overpowered me again. I started crying and breathing heavily. I started repeating terrible words about myself in my head or in a whisper to myself. I hit my head against the wall. The bell rang. Great. I continued to walk, waiting for myself to calm down, and that's when the very bad part happened.

The class that Luke had second hour was going to the school forest for that class period. The class walked by me and I made eye contact with Luke. *Babe, I love you. Please, talk to me, give me a hug, anything. What did I do wrong?* Then, he looked away and kept walking. That's where it all went wrong. I wiped my tears away and held my breath. Time to go to class.

I walked in and felt like shit. I didn't talk to anyone or even pay attention. I just wanted to go home or go back in time. One of the two would be great. I wanted my boyfriend, but it didn't feel the same anymore. I trudged throughout the class, begging for everything to be okay again. *Why today?*

Why here? Why does this have to happen? Why am I such a screw-up? I just want my life back. I want to be a normal kid again, I want to not have to battle with myself over simple situations. Please, I want to be a normal kid. I'm so tired of convincing myself every single day that I am good enough. I want to be fully convinced. Please, I want my life back. Please…

After the bell finally rang, I walked out. Luke and I didn't talk in the halls as much as I'd like, but we did indeed talk. So, I'll take it. He noticed that I was sad, and tried to get me to tell him. I somewhat told him. Then, I walked him to his class and walked across the school to mine. I then stepped into the noisy classroom and felt overwhelmed. It was an overload of power, and I couldn't take it.

"Can we talk?" I desperately asked my friend Seth.

"Yeah, of course."

"Not here, out in the hall."

"One second," he replied, "I'll ask."

I am usually good at getting out of situations, so I said that I wanted to ask.

"No, I want to." Seth insisted. So, he walked over to the choir teacher.

"Can we go talk out in the hall?"

"Um, for what?" My instructor asked hesitantly.

"To talk."

"So, that someone doesn't die." I interrupted.

"Um, what?" My confused choir teacher pondered.

With that, I made Seth walk out into the hall with me. I was expecting to talk for just a couple minutes to explain what was on my mind. So, we walked around the halls just talking and laughing about life. I felt way better. He didn't even really talk, as in give me advice or feedback, he just listened. I needed that. We ended up spending most of the class time talking, but it was well overdue. I loved it. He always can clear my mind. I'm very thankful for him. So, yeah, we spent most of the class making laps around the halls, again, I felt better.

Next, I had Civics for fourth period. Great. One of my friends named Emily informs me that my other friend Heidi was telling people some nasty secrets about me. It angered me a lot. Once I saw Luke, I yelled at him and walked away. I missed him. I missed us. He followed me. I was going to cry. He stood by me and I was actually very happy that he stayed with me. I needed him. He cared. Oh my god, he cared.

We both knew the bell was going to ring and I mentioned it. I didn't want him to, but I told him to go to class, so he wasn't late. I was wishing in my head that he would stay, because at this point in time I was crying. I didn't want to be left alone. But he nodded and walked away. *Babe, I need you right now.* I better try to go to class. I started walking, about 20 seconds after Luke left, and tried to stop crying.

I got somewhat of a handle on my emotions and I trudged into class. I could feel it again. Are you kidding me? I've never had more than one panic attack in a day, never the less three. How is that even possible? The tears started forming around my eyes. Don't blink don't blink. Oh no, the teacher is looking at me. Did she notice? The teacher walks over towards me.

"Are you okay?" she asks.

"No."

This is the same teacher that I told I wanted to kill myself to in the past. I'm pretty close with her outside of school, but I couldn't talk to her. I am not even comfortable writing about it to you guys. I want to keep it private. So, I told her I couldn't talk to her. I asked if I could go walk around the halls for a couple minutes and she accepted my request. Then, I asked if Seth could walk with me, too.

She also accepted that. Seth and I started walking and the principal met us around the corner.

"Um, what are you doing?" She demanded, very snotty.

"Mrs. V said that we could walk around." I said, trying to remain calm.

"Why?"

"So that someone doesn't die." I then turned away. I really dislike this lady.

"Camryn, what do you mean?"

"Me." I didn't want to talk to her at all.

"So, you're saying you have to talk, and Ms. V said you could go out in the hall?"

Wow, what the hell is this lady smoking? How did she get that out of someone dying? Oh well, I don't want to talk to her.

I sarcastically yell, "Sure." with my hands up and turn away from her bullshit.

I then see Luke walking up behind her and towards me. I turned away from him and walked with Seth. I could feel the tears forming, I ran my back into my locker and held up my hair.

"It's all going to start again." I was talking myself into being sad.

Camryn, shut up. You're talking yourself into this. Luke catches up to us and tries to grab my wrists. I felt like my whole world was crumbling. I wanted this to be over. I'm sick of life sucking. When is something good going to happen? When is something great going to come out of this? Probably never. I am a waste of space.

"Babe. It'll be okay." My reassuring boyfriend promised me.

"No, no it won't. It's all going to start again. Everyone is going to make fun of me. Everyone is going to turn against me." I was certain. There was zero doubt in my mind. I knew that everyone was going to tease me and in the moment, I let it ruin everything. I wanted to die. Everything was going downhill. Then the bitchy principal appeared around the corner once again. She just loved ruining people's days, I guess. She said we couldn't be in the halls. That pissed me off a lot. I was having a mental breakdown and she was trying to make me feel guilty for something that I can't control. Oooh, she angers me. It would be different if she maybe tried to help, but she didn't. Instead of asking if I was okay, she asked why I was in the halls. Instead of offering a safe place to cry, she told me to get back to class. I couldn't. I couldn't go back to class. In my mind, that was the worst possible thing. To go back to class and learn about something stupid that I didn't care about and let my thoughts eat me alive. I couldn't cry in class, but I needed to let everything out because it's all been bottled up for a long time. Everything just felt so horrible. I was powerless. I needed to cry, it would hurt so bad to stop. To cry, I need to be alone.

I refused to go back to class, because honestly, I couldn't. I needed to get all of the emotions out. I needed to feel something. She wouldn't let me. I kept refusing. I've been respectful my entire life, but now I felt that I had to stand up for myself. I would respect her, but then again, I need to help myself. I won't put her stupid needs over mine in this situation.

So, after arguing, she allowed the three of us to go into the conference room. Thank you. We had a couple minutes to talk. I basically just yelled at Luke, even though I should have been talking to Seth. He actually helps me with my problems. He'd make me feel like everything is going to be okay again. I needed that; yet, I chose the negative solution.

I wish that everyone had a Seth. The world would be a lot better. I don't know what I'd do without him. You wouldn't be reading this book right now. I wouldn't be breathing right now. If you have a Seth, don't let go. People like Seth are hard to find.

Then, I went to class and began to write this. Right now, I am completely against the teachers in my school. I need to be alone right now. I need to be in a quiet area with no judgy eyes on me. I need to gather my thoughts, catch my breath, and I'll be fine. I wish that they would understand that. I wish they could be in my shoes so they could see that's all that I need. Alone time. Five minutes. Five minutes is all I want to just calm down. It's all I need. So, please, just let me be, okay?

But no. My notes are more important than my mental health. They are more important than my well being. A letter on a fucking piece of paper is more important, because we let that control our entire future. Ever heard, "Everybody is genius. But if you judge a fish by its ability to climb a tree, it will live its whole life believing that it is stupid." - Albert Einstein. I love it. Because it's true.

School. Well, we all have different opinions about school. Mine, I dislike the way schools are run very, very much. I believe that a lot of classes that we students take are dumb. This is my opinion; you don't have to agree with me at all. Basic math, that is important. We'll need that for a lot of things in our adult lives. Addition, subtraction, you know, that's very important. Along with fractions, decimals, and other simple things like that. Basic math, even algebra one, but everything above that, most people don't use that in their daily life. Pound in the basic classes we take up until high school. I took algebra one as an eighth grader, which is important too.

So, once we get into high school, I think things should be different. See, we learned about the civil rights, we learned how to divide fractions, we learned the difference between a revolution and rotation of Earth, but now it's go time. The last four years of student's high school careers should be chosen by the individual. Since kindergarten, we were forced to know our career path. Do research so we knew the income, schooling, and skill requirements. Do something with that.

I'm going to use my boyfriend for an example. Luke, well, by his test scores, people would label him stupid. These past year that I've gotten to know him, I know for a fact that he is not stupid at all. Now, I absolutely love that quote from Albert Einstein because it's so true. Luke isn't amazing at math, but boy that kid is a genius when it comes to anything about cars. He knows just about everything under the sun about fixing things, kinds of cars, what part goes where. I honestly know shit about the topic. Sure, I know a couple car names that I like. I know brands, but I'm super far from knowing as much as he does.

He's just so smart. Until he gets his state test scores back. Then he thinks he's stupid. When his teachers talk to him like he knows nothing, he forgets that he, in fact, is a genius. We test him on things that he isn't passionate about. We test him on things he won't conform into his future. He won't use a lot of the things you're throwing at him.

My boyfriend honestly and truly believes that he is stupid. He's not even close to being stupid, the school system just tells him that. The school system doesn't care, they just want good grades. What if it were vice-versa? What if I got a test handed to me about car parts and I had no interest in being an auto mechanic of any kind? You see, we treat everyone as a whole and expect them to all get the same thing out of it. This really is an individual thing. We can't just expect the same from everyone. Everyone feels dumb. If someone is going to grow up to be a mathematician, by all means, go for it. Take all of those math classes. If that's your cup of tea, go for it. Me on the other hand, I won't need to use all of those big math problems. But yet, I still have I take them.

XXXVIII

So, I've told you a lot about my opinion of how schools are run. Obviously, I hate it. I really do. At least my school anyways. I live in a small town in Northwest Wisconsin. Yes, I am back at my original school. I thought maybe things would be different, and they are. I have barely any drama. Most of that being that I made new friends. Most of my friends are guys, and I often get called names for that, but it's just proving my point as to why I am friends with the boys. No drama = happy Camryn. Half way through the first quarter of my freshman year, and I don't recall any drama at all besides with my boyfriend. I'll take that any day.

I do have only one close friend at school but really, it's quality, not quantity. I would rather have Seth (the greatest friend I've ever had) than the close friends that I had in my past. Sure, they're good people, but nothing can compare to my best friend. He's the best. So, although it gets rough having one close friend at school, I would rather have one amazing friend over 50 fake friends any day.

Anyways, yeah, I really dislike school - mostly math classes - and it's really hard for me to do good in school. My whole life I was a straight A student, until Jr. High. When I got depression, it sucked all of the motivation out of me. I had no drive to maintain my good grades or my parent's pride anymore. I wish that I could be that way again. Of course I could, it's just so hard for me to get back up. Everytime I say to myself, "Camryn, let's do our civics homework." I know that I need to do it. I really do. I want to. I want to make my teachers and parents proud. I want to shock them so bad. I want to show them what I can do. But most of all, I want to show myself that I can do this.

It's just so difficult for several reasons. For starters, I already brought up depression. Now, I'm not just blaming it on this. On one hand, yes, I do believe that depression played a major part on my drive and motivational status. It not only destroyed the idea of school for me, but also, sports, family events, going out to eat, going to hang out with friends. The excitement for those activities changed.

I didn't like this change. I wanted my life back. I wanted to be me. Yet getting depression changed so much for me. For most of those things that I listed, I was able to bounce back up and find my way back to loving them. School, well, that's a different story. Besides depression, I blame myself mostly for this. Sure, depression started it, but I should be able to push myself to achieve my goals. I'm lazy.

I will not say that any of this isn't my fault, because it is. A lot of the reasoning behind it being my fault is my opinions. For example, you reading this would probably imagine that I'm a pretty smart girl. I mean, I've been told that I'm a great writer and here you are now, reading my book. You haven't seen my grades yet though.

I mean, that's what defines our intelligence, isn't it? I, along with every single other student, am graded on how well we can remember things. I don't get graded on how well I can save someone's life, I get graded on how well I can name if a shape is congruent or how a function on a graph works.

The teachers, they look at the gradebook and say, "Yep, she's stupid." Just because my grades don't scream intelligence. They look at my test scores and wonder why I get bad grades, if I'm above average. I disagree with the school system.

Today, I walked out of my least favorite class because I could feel my face getting hot, I could feel my breathing getting heavier, I could feel the judgmental students staring at me. I did what was best for me, and got out of there. I just needed a quick breather and I'd be fine. So, I walked down the hall to see if the guidance counselor was there, she wasn't. Okay, let's go into the office. No one was there. Dang it.

So, I went back to class. I calmed down a lot just being out of that hell hole. I walked back in and the teacher followed me to my desk. Immediately, she started bitching at me, saying I can't just leave. She didn't understand. All of my teachers knew about me. They knew about my mental health issues, and I have permission from all teachers to take a quick breather if I'm feeling overwhelmed. Nothing extreme, just take a lap around the hall and come back in when ready. I rarely ever need to do that though, mostly because I'm scared that I'll get

yelled at. Everyone offered the option.
Everyone showed that they somewhat care
about my mental health, besides one.

Yes, my algebra teacher. I took
algebra one as an eighth grader, but
I'm taking it again because I missed a
lot of concepts while being in the
hospital towards the end of the year. I
always got teased in her class. I was
called dumb a lot, even though I was in
advanced math. Confusing, right? I'm a
smart girl. Math isn't really my thing,
but my test scores say differently. I
must be a good guesser, I don't know.

I'm not the best at grasping
concepts right away. I'm better with
one on one teaching. So, when I'd go
for help, I felt stupid. Not only did
students tease me, but my teacher made
me feel like a complete idiot. She
talked to me like I was the dumbest

person alive. She usually just ignored me when I'd ask for help. When she did attempt to help, she treated me like I had the mental capacity of a first grader. She didn't help, yet she preached in class discussion that asking questions are okay; even though for her, it's not. For her class anyways. She made me feel worthless.

So, what do you think that I did? I stopped trying. I didn't do my homework, I didn't participate in class, I didn't pay attention. I didn't care anymore. To me, there was no use. I already have myself trying to convince myself that there's no point in trying, but I overcame that. Then, my own teacher wouldn't even help me. I was powerless. What's the point? To this day, I don't try. I really wish I did. I want to. It's just so hard.

Myself being no help is one thing, but the teachers being no help is another.

I wish they understood. This isn't how schooling should be. Teachers should help, teachers should encourage students to do good. No, not all teachers are like my math teacher, but a shit ton are. I hate that so much. I always thought that I was smart. Always. I believed it, but once I got into Jr. High, I stopped believing that I was smart. I stopped believing in myself.

I know several teachers that look out for me, but most don't. Especially my math teacher. She was just yelling at me for going into the hall. I mean, I see why she'd be concerned, if she even was - if she was, she had a funny way of showing it - I mean, I didn't even tell her where I was going. And I would have, but I couldn't. I was about to blow. I had to leave so I wouldn't disrupt class. My teacher saw it as an act of being disrespectful. Again, lack of knowledge, having people act out in the wrong way. I don't think that my math teacher purposely tries to ruin my life, she just doesn't understand. I wish everyone understood. I wish people weren't such inconsiderate assholes, but you know, it's life. Have to deal with it.

So, I listened to my teacher nag at me and then sat down. She returns only moments from walking away, and tells me to just go to the office. I was so confused. I told her I just needed a break and she comes back and tells me to go to the office. She calls my random acts, of something I can't control "disrespectful" but doesn't give two shits about something that I needed to do. I just didn't want to make a scene. I didn't want to take away from graphing stupid formulas. So, I just went out to catch my breath and gather my thoughts. I would return shortly and be fine again. But no, I got sent to the office. I love the secretary there at least, so that's a bonus. I put all my stuff together, and my teacher went to call the office.

"At least I don't have to be in this hell hole anymore." I mumbled to my desk partner.

After that, I walked down to the office. The amazing lady behind the desk asked if I was okay. I said yes, and grabbed my phone. I texted my mom and told her to call the office, because I got in trouble. She kind of freaked out, but moments after texting her, the principal came out of her office. Oh gosh, not this. She stares at me. I thought that she was going to yell at me for having my phone out, because we weren't allowed to have them out during school. Instead, she just asked if I was going home. I said no, respectfully. She asked me why I was there. I told her that my teacher likes using things against me and she freaked out and tried to turn it into a life lesson. Whatever.

I waited for about ten minutes, then she called me into her office. In my mind, I told myself not to argue; no matter how stupid the things she said were. I didn't need to get in trouble with the principal, again. So, she explained that I needed to fix my behavior and I nodded. Then, she said the most idiotic thing I ever heard anyone say. She straight up told me that I need to stop having anxiety attacks. Well, Mrs. Butt Head, I don't know what fantasy world you're living in where you think that I can control these, but you're getting on my nerves. She told me that if I am going to have one, I should at least be respectful enough to tell the teacher.

First off, anxiety and panic attacks don't just happen when you're overwhelmed or nervous. They can happen at any given moment, so it's not like you always know when you're going to have one. I usually can tell, because I mostly have them when I'm overwhelmed. A lot of people have no idea when they will hit.

Boy, did that piss me off. Oh yeah, I fucking chose to have this. I chose not to be able to have confidence to do what I want, I choose to be scared over simple situations, I choose to make a fool out of myself. Makes perfect sense! Just because you chose to be a bitch, doesn't mean that I chose to be "disrespectful." I was doing something that was best for me and was just getting beat down for it. I don't see anything wrong with it. Sure, getting up and walking out of class isn't a good thing, but after I would explain to my teacher that I just didn't want to disrupt class, I would see it being okay. I guess not. It's the end of the world. At the end of the day, my grades are more important than my mental health. I think that's stupid. Really stupid. If I die, oh well, as long as I die with no missing assignments, I'm good.

No, grades really are the last thing on my mind right now. My whole life, I've been preached to about how important grades are, so I tried so hard to impress everyone. I tried so hard to have a future. My parents were always proud of me for that. Soon, it just was, how I was. A smart girl. I was a goodie-goodie. I never ever got in trouble. If a teacher even raised their voice at me, or called me out during a class discussion, I would probably cry. I never even wrote anything on my paper, but my name, the date, and the answers. I never doodled, I never scribbled. I did my homework and life was good. I had good friends and proud parents, perfect.

Once seventh grade hit, you know the story. But the thing was, everyone says how important grades are for your future. But, with depression, you don't see your future. To me, it was useless to do my homework because I was going to die before I got there anyways. I never thought of myself ever graduating. I never thought about myself getting my first car. It was always just blank, if I tried to think about my future after seventh grade. It was useless. I stopped trying. I literally gave zero effort. My paper had doodles on it and my brain had scribbles in it. There was nothing but negativity on my mind. So, seriously, homework wasn't number one. I was going to die anyways, so what's the point? My last thoughts won't be, "Oh shit, I should have done that math homework!" It will probably be, "Oh shit, I should have written more to my mom!" So, you see, I don't give two shits about my homework right now. I was content on trying to save myself.

XXXIX

Well, here we are, writing about something that I never thought I'd have to write about. I lost my best friend. My best friend. I love him to death, honestly, I do. I tried so hard to be a good friend to him, and I thought that I did. Seth, well, he made me feel good about myself. Really good about myself. He always told me how much I meant to him and it felt so good to hear stuff like that from someone, and I tried to return the favor the best that I could. I meant everything that I said to him too. He did mean the world to me. I was very grateful for him.

Everyone should have someone like him in their life, the world would be a much better place if that were true. Everyone would feel loved. Everyone would hear the words that they deserve to be told. People would be happier, people would be nicer. The world would be a better place for everyone, it would be beautiful. I lost mine. I really wish everything was the same, more than anything honestly.

I miss him. It's only been a couple days, but it feels like it's been years. Seeing him in the halls breaks my heart. I wish that I could just go up and hug him. I wish we could go to my house and talk about anything, because that's how we are. We always can talk about anything. We used to be able to tell each other anything and everything, and I needed that. He needed that; everyone needs it. But it's gone.

I'll tell you why. So, Seth, he was probably the only person in this world who thought that I was perfect. I know that I am far from perfect by a long shot. Heck, everyone knows that… Besides him. It felt really good because I thought that I was no better than a piece of poop, but he saw me as this amazing thing and he just helped me so much. He's the reason that I want to live - he's the reason that I'm alive.

The reason that I'm writing this book, is him. This book started off being a writing assignment for my English teacher. One day, I let my guidance counselor read it and she said that she would like to publish it or use it in a counselor magazine or something. I thought that was pretty amazing, so I put a lot of thought into it. Deep down, I really wanted to help, I really wanted to be known, but I didn't know that. Seth, he believed in me from the start. He encouraged me to keep writing and see how far I would get with this.

The thing was, I was jumping up and down on the inside because I felt recognized. Someone noticed me. My writing. I wanted someone to show me excitement or pride, because I was proud of myself. Hell, I was so proud of myself. I wanted to share it with someone. I wanted someone to say that they were proud of me. I wanted someone to jump up and down and hug me. But no one did. My mom seemed annoyed with it when I brought up the idea of me writing a book or getting part of my writing published. Sure, she probably was proud, but she didn't make me feel like she was. No one did. I told people and they were just like, "Oh, that's cool."

So, I started to just give up on the idea of me becoming a writer. I mean, no one showed any support, so it must not be possible. I am a screwup. I told Seth that I gave up and he freaked out and told me that I was an amazing writer and I needed to keep going. Ah, there it is. My best friend to the rescue once again. So, here we are now. Pretty funny.

Since then, I've contemplated giving up many times on my writing. I've even deleted my book on occasion. Luckily, Seth is way ahead of the game and he made a new copy every single day. Seth saw how talented I was from the start, and he believed in me.

I never thought that we would part, honestly. I thought that we would

always be in each other's lives. I
hoped so. So, what changed? This school
year was just all messed up. Seth
changed big time. I don't know, I think
he realized how imperfect I really was,
just like everyone else did.

This year we got a new student
named Kayli. She's beautiful inside and
out and I'd really love to be better
friends with her. Since she came, Seth
started becoming distant with me. He
started going to her with his problems
and stopped talking to me. It hurt
really bad, but I was happy he had
another person in his life to help him.
He deserved the world.

After a while, Seth completely
changed in the way that he talked to
me. He no longer really tried at all.
He no longer supported me if I wanted
to give up. Seth always would chase

after me if I walked away. Seth would always try and talk me out of suicide and it worked, obviously. But then he stopped. Instead of trying to stop me, he would just say something like, "No." and then not talk to me. He was gone. I lost my reason to live. I lost my support. Whenever I'd bring it up to him, he'd say that he was still here, and physically, I guess that he was. Emotionally, his support was gone. He no longer called me beautiful or important. He no longer texted me to check on me and eventually, we weren't in each other's lives anymore. It hurts so bad. I never, ever, imagined that I'd lose him. But here we are. Alone. I'm alone in this battle once again. I just hope Seth gets everything he wants, because he deserves it. I miss him and love him, but I want what's best for him, even if it's not me. That's what gets me. How can someone be best for you, but you're not best for them? Some things are really messed up in this world.

XL

I'm so lost. I haven't felt this way in a long time. I don't remember the last time that I felt like this honestly. I don't know, I feel trapped. I'm alone and it's a weird feeling. I physically have people by my side, true, but that's not the same as having emotional support and love and care. It's far from being the same. If it was, I'd be doing just fine. There's people all around me obviously. I'm in health class right now and there's a bunch of people in here. But that doesn't make it better. That doesn't help me. Even some of the people in this class have said that they will be there for me. Even some people say that I can go to them, but how many mean it? None. No one. I feel like poop right now honestly. I miss my best friend more than anything. Oh well, I still have to keep going. I just wish life was better for me right now. It's been decent lately. Mentally, I've been doing great, I haven't really been thinking suicidal, I haven't cut, and I've been positive for the most part. It's just getting really bad again and I don't know what to do. I want to give up again. I really do, but I have to accomplish my biggest goal; completing my book.

It's still October 10th. I keep looking at Seth and my heart hurts really bad. I love him alot and not being able to call him my friend hurts so bad. He's doing just fine without me. Way different than all of the times he described what would happen if he lost me. Life just seems to be perfect for him, and life is a living hell for me. It figures. I'm stupid for thinking that it was impossible for myself to matter. I'm stupid for thinking he actually meant everything that he said. I'm just an idiot. A huge idiot. I'm a screw up. I really wonder how in the world I thought that someone could actually care about me.

XLI

It's now the 11th, this day is absolutely terrible. Life was going really good, and it just goes down so fast, I hate it. I really do. So guys, this time, I was mean to someone else. Wow, what? I was mean to someone? Yes, I said something very mean to someone, and I regret it. I did from the start. I was speaking out in anger, and I really didn't think before I did it. I did something stupid. I mean, why should you believe me now? Everything that I said must be a lie… No, I know what I said was wrong. That doesn't make the situation better, but I know that it was wrong. I wouldn't want that said to me, yet I said it to someone else.

You guys know that I'm a very nice person, obviously. You reading this know me better than anyone. I write down a lot in here, but I don't really tell anyone my problems. This is my go-to. So, you know a lot about me. I'd say that I'm a good person overall. Of course, I make mistakes, but who doesn't? So, I will admit, I made a mistake. It was wrong and I regret saying it a lot. But you see, this situation just went up in flames.

Let's start at the beginning. So, it was the day of homecoming. Luke and I just recently got back together as you know. The thing is, Luke started hiding his phone in the truck.. Which is whatever, I don't really care. Luke has my phone password, Instagram password, Snapchat password, Facebook password and more. He's able to check my phone whenever. I don't really care. It's not like I have anything to hide from him. But I don't know anything about his phone. Since I was younger, I said I never would want my boyfriends passwords or anything. If I was dating someone, that would mean I trust them. Trust is the most important thing aside from communication, right? I was kind of curious to why our relationship was like that. He hides everything from me, but I am completely open to anything and everything to him. It's just how I am. Maybe Luke is the kind of guy who likes to keep everything private, but then why does he want so different from me?

I don't know, it was starting to bother me. If I was busy doing something like showering or doing chores for my mom for a couple minutes, he was on my phone checking my messages. But god forbid me even pick up his phone to hand it to him. He got really awkward around me if I was next to it or handing it to him. I never had the desire to go through his phone. I was just wondering why he was so weird about it.

My mind was telling me a lot of stuff I really didn't want to hear. The biggest thing was obviously, "He's cheating on you." I didn't really want to believe it. Who would though? He couldn't be cheating on me. I would've found out by now, right? My thoughts were racing with ideas, and I began the difficult process of overthinking.

XLII

Shell Lake homecoming. That should be fun. This particular day, the event was Powder Puff Football. So, I sat next to Luke. We laughed and had a good time as usual. He makes me so happy. I decided to test him. Like I said, I had no desire to check his phone. I just wanted to see how he'd react if I requested the same thing as he requests from me. So, with that being said, I said, "Hey, do you want to switch phones for the night?" And he completely overreacted. He kept asking why, and saying no; he was super nervous about it. Well, that's the reaction I was not hoping for. I got scared… He must be hiding something, right? I didn't care to go through his pictures or texts with his dad, I just wanted to see how he would react if I asked the same things that he asked of me.

After the football games, it led to a huge argument. I didn't want it to, it just ended up that way. In the car, I asked him why he wouldn't let me see his phone. He didn't really know how to answer. So, I got angry that he couldn't answer it. I brought up him cheating and he screamed that he would never do anything like that because he knows how it feels. He's mentioned several times that he never would cheat on someone; never has, never will.

I half believed him. I mean, there were a lot of rumors that he cheated on his last girlfriend, Miranda, a lot. I believed it somewhat. The first time I heard it was from two good friends of mine in my grade, and it was when we first started dating. I asked him about it, and he denied ever cheating on anyone. Must just be a rumor.

I know Miranda likes to make up a lot of crap. She's basically called me every name in the book. I've never been on good terms with her. I remember getting in my first argument on social media with her. I was really young. I got a Facebook in like first grade or something like that. That was my super, super, super annoying phase. I literally updated my status constantly, and I was the type of person that I get annoyed with easily today.

One day, my fourth generation iPod broke and I made it sound like it was the end of the world. I was obviously being sarcastic, saying that I didn't know what I was going to do. Now, Miranda is two years older than me. She was in about third-fourth grade and she decided to pick a fight with me over that.

Although, yes it was a stupid post. I mean, I was like seven or eight or something around there, and she started calling me, and I quote, "The stupidest person ever." That broke my first grade heart. So, since then, she's done little things to try and kick me down. It wasn't common. It didn't happen frequently, I'll give her that, but still, we never were on good terms. I could go on and tell you about certain situations, but I don't really feel the need to. It was the past and I don't let it get to me anymore.

She often would come up in a lot of the problems I would face. Note, she never had the guts to say any of it to my face. She always told a person - her cousin Heidi, who I've mentioned a lot recently - and that person always told me. I probably know more that she's said about me than she thinks, but trust me, it's not pretty. Her name has always made me cringe. I'm not like her, though. I don't try to ruin her life. I don't get joy out of things like that. Oh well.

Luke hates her. From what he has told me, she treated him terribly. She cheated on him a lot and always made him feel guilty about the the things he loved. For instance, Luke loves going to car shows with his dad. I know that they really bond over it. When Luke and Miranda were dating, she never would let him go to any car shows. Heck, she didn't even let him hug his own cousin.

I wasn't the only person she treated like crap, I guess. Heidi has also told me a million stories about things Miranda does to her. As you can see, we never have really liked each other. When I heard people telling me that Luke cheated on her when we were dating, I took it into consideration. Then, when he'd tell me that he never did, I trusted him. I know how she likes ruining people's lives, she probably just made it up to get dirt on Luke. But, you never know. I didn't know anything about Luke at all before we met at State Ice Fishing, so it very well could be that Luke cheated on Miranda.

The thought of him cheating was always in the back of my mind. The voices stepped forward at random moments and say, "He's cheating on you." All of the time. I ignored it, and did my best not to think about it a

357

lot, but it was difficult. I had a pretty good handle on it, until Luke started being really secretive around me. Then, when he said that I couldn't see his phone, I got bad vibes. Could he be cheating on me?

The next day, everything was fine again. I didn't bring it up to him, and we were fine. But I told him that I was going to delete all of the guys off of my snapchat. He liked that idea, and told me that he was going to delete all of the girls, with the exception of some. I never asked him to, but it made me feel a lot better. I never, ever break promises, and he made me promise that I blocked everyone, but some, and I did. So, I asked him. He promised, and named the girls that he didn't. I was okay with that, and we both were satisfied. Tomorrow would be the homecoming dance. I was going with Luke and I was very excited.

XLIII

That morning, I woke up and started getting ready. Luke and I were going out to eat, and I was super excited. We were going to reenact the first thing we ate together. At state, we both got a large chocolate shake, and I got curly fries at Arby's. He got some weird combination of fries and other stuff in a bowl and my mom laughed at how weird we were. Our plan was to go to Arby's and order that, just for laughs.

I was excited, we rarely went out to eat, and the idea of us doing that was super cute. Making things even better, it was his idea. So, he came over and we laughed and I made him shower at my house because he was stanky. I went downstairs, happy with where life was.

Then, I saw his phone on my bed. I've seen him put in his password before, it's just a quick swipe. Should I? The thoughts keep pushing me to, but I know that it's wrong. Wait… Is it wrong? I mean, yes, it is. I would be going on his phone without permission; it's an invasion of privacy. But I felt like I needed to.

I went on it. I went on his snapchat, he didn't block anyone. He had every girl on there and talked to a lot of them. Oh, he promised he never talked to anyone. I got a little suspicious. I didn't read their messages, but I probably should have. Next, I went into Facebook Messenger. Again, a lot of girls were there. I didn't really care, until I saw two girls that I know like him. Hmm, should I read their messages? Nah, I trust him.

Then I see it. He was talking to Miranda. Well, what the hell. All that he says about her is how much he hates her and wants nothing to do with her.

I decided to read that one. Wow, they talk a lot. Nothing like people who "hate" each other. As I read, I was really shocked. He gave her his number, and said to text that instead.

Things got worse from from there. I found out that he was going over to her house. Tears rolled down my face… We were dating during this. Miranda also had a boyfriend. What the fuck? All he ever said was he hated her and how terrible of a person she was. And then I see something even more disappointing than him sneaking over to her house because he, "Couldn't wait to hold her in his arms." Yuck. He said, "Just know, I've always loved you."

Wow. I was speechless. I set his phone on my bed and walked upstairs. I went into the garage where my mom was and said, "He's cheating on me." She was super confused, but I told her to follow me downstairs. I felt like my heart was ripped out and thrown at a cactus a million times. I didn't know what to do. It hurt a lot. It hurt so much guys. So, my mom followed me downstairs and into my bedroom.

"Lock my door." I barked at her. Then I went on his phone and showed her the messages. She pointed out that it started getting worse after he broke up with me the first time. It started off while we were dating, and who the hell knows what went on there? I know about their past as a couple, and what they did, so, I'm a little scared to know what they did together this time.

As soon as her boyfriend dumped her - probably because she was cheating on him, again. - Luke dumped me. But the thing is, Miranda really hates Luke. She never lied about that. I'll explain more on that in a bit.

My mom was as shocked as I was. Out of all the people, and he cheated on me with her? Don't get me wrong, she's nice to most people, I think. She's seriously gorgeous, but on the inside, it's definitely not as beautiful as her face. But he picked her. I felt like going under a rock and disappearing. As I continued to read the messages my heart got heavier and heavier. The first time we broke up, well, at least I know the reason now.

He was with her for a while, then when her boyfriend ended things off, he thought maybe he had a chance, which he didn't, so he broke up with the girl who would have never given up on him. I would do anything for that guy, and I made sure he knew that.

After realizing that Miranda just used him, he went back to me. She was going to make up a whole bunch of stories, according to her friends and Luke. Only I had no idea what their little games were. I had no idea what went on prior to us breaking up. So, I thought maybe he just realized how much I care about him, not that he got rejected. So, we got back together as you know.

We dated for a couple weeks and then he dumped me and had sex with a 24 year old, a couple hours post breaking up. After that, he also went back to Miranda.

I needed to talk to someone. I was gathering all of this in my thoughts. So, I go on snapchat and text Seth, we were still best friends. He would be able to help me, right?

Then I text my friend Heidi and say the same thing: "Luke cheated on me," because we were getting along really good recently. She responded like a total bitch. I was confused. She started freaking out and saying I was a liar and all that. I was just stunned. I seeked support, and she turned around and bit me in the butt. Then, Miranda texts me off of Heidi's phone. She tells me to leave her name out of her mouth, and I'm lying, and how she tried to warn me which is complete bull. So, I innocently told her that I wasn't trying to start drama.

Then, she texted me. Weird, I don't know how she got my number, so I asked Heidi. She said she always had it. Well, alright. So, we talked a little bit and we just had a normal conversation. She told me how Luke always cheated on her and a bunch of stuff about how hurt she was. I felt bad for her. Maybe I was wrong this whole time.

I was still so mad at her though. Her past didn't change what she did to try and hurt me. She was with my boyfriend while she knew we were dating, and they both kept it a secret. I'm not going to say they had sex, because I don't know that. I don't know what went on there, so I won't jump to conclusions. Even if there wasn't sex, I'm still so hurt and angry with both of them. Mostly Luke of course, but still.

My first thought was that she was was doing another thing to try and ruin my life. It wouldn't surprise me. Later, I found out that it was true. After a couple minutes of crying, I went upstairs to curl my hair. Sure, I looked like a naked rat, but I wanted to try and look half decent at least. While getting my hair curled, Luke got done in the shower.

Wow, what was I going to say? I wanted to still go to the dance, just not with him. I didn't have any desire to be with him anymore. If he could cheat on me so easily, I don't want to be with him. If he could cheat on me period, I don't want to be with him. In almost every single relationship that I've been in, I was cheated on. I was not going to let it keep happening over and over again.

So, I made up my mind. I was going to break up with Luke. That was honestly the last thing that I would ever want to do. I love him. I really do a lot. But, I need to do what's best for me, even if it meant giving up on my entire world.

I wanted to hear his side of the story. So, he came out and I didn't say a word. I was starting to cry again, so I covered my face. My mom was right next to me, so he didn't say anything either. We just sat in silence. I wondered if he knew. I had a feeling that he did, because I was in tears and he didn't say a single thing at all. I was very curious. I looked up at him. He's adorable. His ocean eyes are my favorite. Do I really want to give up on this?

The images of him kissing another girl flashed through my head. He no longer looked like the perfect man I saw him as. Something changed. I didn't look at him like I did before. I wasn't losing feelings for him, however, I could feel the loss of respect and trust escaping my body. He chose someone else. I kept repeating it in my head. The voices kept saying things to make me angry. *How many other girls do you think he's been with? You're a waste of space. He was just using you. He wanted to feel loved and have someone do stuff for him, and that's just what you did. He never loved you, who would?* I toughed out the pain until

I could walk downstairs. I didn't know if I should bring it up to him right away. What's the best option?

I don't really remember how it came up, but boy, did I want to smack him in the face. I didn't, I would never do that, but that doesn't mean I didn't want to. So, we yelled back and forth, and I didn't even feel bad for him when he laid on my floor and cried. Usually, my heart would break to see him upset, but I was put through so much more and I wasn't planning on falling into his games again.

I wanted to die. My whole world was falling apart. Miranda got what she wanted. She ruined my life. I wondered if she was happy now? Her cravings were finally obtained, and she could get the satisfaction of seeing me a total wreck. This is what she wanted. Good job Miranda. I hope you're proud of yourself.

I was screaming at Luke pretty bad. I told him I was not going to be with someone that thinks cheating is okay. I was being honest. He kept making excuses and so I told him to stop acting like he's perfect, because now I see that he isn't. Before, every flaw that he had, I fell in love with. It made him, well, him. And I love him.

It really did hurt me to see him like this. He looked about the same as me when he broke up with me. I mean, all I could do was roll in a ball and cry, and that's just what he did. I could tell he was sorry… Sorry for cheating and lying, or sorry for getting caught? I don't know. We talked a lot, and he never once, screamed back. I was yelling almost the whole time though. I needed to get the anger out.

After seeing Luke bawl for 45 minutes and try to get anything out of him, I told him to come sit by me. So, he did. He laid on my chest and I played with his hair. He stuffed his face into me and cried. I just held him. I was a little harsh, but I needed to stand up for myself.

I said - not yelling or screaming - "I'm sorry Luke. We can't be together." You could feel his entire body tense up. He screamed and held me so tight. I thought my heart just literally broke. Me being me, I lifted his head up and wiped his tears away. I tried to reassure him, "Baby, it's gonna be okay. I promise." He shook his head, and stood up.

He grabbed his phone, and dialed something. He was calling someone. After seeming like endless ringing, the person picks up. It sounded like a man, but I couldn't tell. "Dad, I love you." There was a response but I couldn't hear what it was. "I made a big mistake and I'm sorry. I'll always love you." The muffled voice got louder and words were said faster, he was worried. With that, Luke hung up.

He started to walk out the door. I was very confused. I grabbed his hand and brought him down to the floor. Again, I held him. I can't imagine Luke being gone forever. He kept apologizing and calling himself stupid. I didn't say he wasn't, like I normally would, I just listened. He told me he realized how much he loves me. He saw how much I cared about him and he never wants to lose me. He told me he wanted to marry me. I just held him and kept my mouth shut. He continued to talk, and after a while, I just told him that I was sorry. The tears rolled down his face, and the screams emerged from his mouth. He just kept rubbing my hair and telling me that he loved me. He started hitting himself and saying that he doesn't know why he's alive. I grabbed his hands and just held him. I didn't want him to hurt himself... I love him too much for that.

Most people would tell me later on that what I just did was the most idiioitc thing I could have done, but I don't care. It was my choice and I feel like I made the right one. I love Luke. I told him that, and he continued to cry. I told him that I can't be cheated on again, he lifted his head up and repeated, "I won't baby, I won't. I promise." Of course, I didn't believe him. He did, and had no problem with it.. So, what's stopping him from doing it again?

XLIV

After talking it over, I asked him, "Do you believe that we can get through this?" His body loosened, and he screamed again but it wasn't sorrow, it was relief. He said the word yes in the happiest cry I've ever heard. I told him that this was for real his last chance. If he thinks that he can dump me just to have sex with another girl because he's not patient enough to wait for me, screw that. I also told him, that if he had the intentions to just ignore everything I said and cheat on me again, then he could just walk away and leave me alone because I am not going to let him do that. He just explained how badly he wants us to have a future together and he won't ever do it again.

And with that said, I told him to get ready. Our plans for going out to eat were soiled due to the time now. He got dressed and said he had to bring his truck to his dad real quick. I said okay, and got ready myself.

Then, after a couple minutes of talking with Heidi and Miranda, they showed up. I really didn't want them there. The house was a complete mess and I just wanted to be alone. They said that they were here to cheer me up. Bull crap "cheer me up." If I had an affair with someone's boyfriend while they had a girlfriend, the last thing that I'd do would be go see her. I'd be different if she didn't know Luke and I were dating, but she did. She went there to rub it in my face.

I just wanted them to leave. They probably would when Luke showed up. She continued to tell me a lot about Luke, and it was making me angry. If any of what she was telling me was true, I don't even want to try and make it work with him. After about a half an hour, Luke returns. Thank god. I was right. They left shortly after he came in. I didn't even want to bring any of it up to him yet.

I wanted to have fun at my first homecoming. So, we got ready. I ended up having a great night with the man that I love. Seth was different though. He completely ignored me every time I tried to talk to him. Oh well, I danced with my other friends and boyfriend and had a blast.

XLV

You are probably wondering how that story ties in with how I was mean to someone. Well, I was just giving you a little background information. This is now about the mistake itself. So, if you have any form of social media at all, you most likely know what the #Huh challenge is. I've been seeing them for a while now, and some of them are funny, but others are just plain mean.

My boyfriend was over and he, my sister, and I were all sitting upstairs. We wanted food, but we didn't really have anything to eat. Then I remembered that I had $20 and insisted that Luke take us to McDonald's so I could buy us some grub. He accepted and my sister kept trying to make some roasts but failed. Turns out, I'm really good at them. I was mostly roasting Luke. He's a good sport and could share a laugh with us. My favorite was, "My name is Luke and I cheat on my girlfriend, because the only thing I'm good at playing with is her heart, huuuuh." I was on a roll roasting Luke. No matter how hard Violet and Luke tried, they both sucked at them. I on the other hand, just had them keep coming up in my head. We all laughed so hard and it was the first time in awhile that I was feeling decent.

So, we get to McDonald's and guess who's working? You guessed it, Miranda. I continued to make jokes about Luke, and they continued to laugh. I stopped when Luke said the orders, though. Miranda was getting a little cranky with us. Once we got up to the window, she called us rude and we drove off.

My sister knows how much Miranda has done to me my whole life, so she told me to make one about Miranda. I thought of one that was really mean and I hesitated to say it, because it was so mean, guys. This time, I recorded it. I mentioned that I deleted over 500 people on snapchat recently; boys and girls that I didn't want/need. I just had mostly close friends, people that I've talked out of suicide or come to me for help. Otherwise, I deleted a lot of people.

So, I was putting the roasts on my story. Everyone thought that they were hilarious. Then I made the mistake. Saying mean things about a person is one thing, but posting it on social media is a complete other. In the moment, I didn't think about how Miranda would feel if she heard this. I was selfish, and with that, I said the most mean thing that I have ever said about someone. "My name's Miranda and I wear baggy sweatshirts to cover up the fact that I look like I'm pregnant with triplets."

That's right, I was an asshole. Take it in. Be disappointed in me. I'm disappointed in me, too. What I said was wrong, and I understand that. I do. I knew it from the start, and I don't even know why I said it, honestly.

So, the next day basically the entire school is in uproar. That situation, that tiny part of me, is what I'm labeled as. Only they completely changed what I said. So, I called her fat. And yes, that was a very poor choice of mine. I regret even saying it. It's not me.

It's very out of character for me. I mean, I am a good person. I honestly and truly think that. I've saved so many lives, guys. I have, and I'm so proud of myself. I'm doing what I love. I'm helping people. I compliment people, I try to make them feel good. I love to make people feel good.

Seriously, I do. It's my favorite thing in the world. I'm not just saying that either.

I love making a positive impact in people's lives. That's why this 14 year old is writing an autobiography. I could be riding four wheeler or watching TV, but instead I'm writing this. Don't get me wrong, I love those things. But I love helping people more.

So, perfect. I get to write, and help people. What's better than that? Nothing. Honestly, nothing gives me the same satisfaction as helping people. I'm being honest. I don't care what I'm doing, as long as I'm helping. I just love it. It's hard to put into words. If you are as passionate about something as I am passionate about helping people, then you completely know the feeling. It's amazing.

I don't know what I'd do if I couldn't help people. I don't know what I did before. Well, I felt worthless and out of place. I didn't know why I was put on this earth. I tried so hard to find talents, but I couldn't. But now, I can see it. I can see my talents, and I'm so proud of myself. Being a good person is all that I have. I would be nothing if I didn't try my best to help people. I would feel empty.

So, I think that I'm a good person. I really do. But because of a mistake I made, none of it matters. Me, staying up until 3am on the phone with a stranger every single night, that doesn't matter. Me, having a great time with my family, but hearing my phone ring, and seeing a number I don't recognize, calling out, "Be right back, I gotta save a life." and walking out. That doesn't matter. Falling asleep in class because I stayed up telling someone how important and beautiful they are, knowing they had a gun up to their head, that doesn't matter. This is all worth it to me. I love helping them, because everyone deserves to know their worth, everyone. And in this world we live in, not everyone knows or gets told. So, I will try to be that person.

But none of that matters. I disrespected one person, so that's what defines me. Everyone is calling me a bad person and a bully. But the thing is, I called Miranda fat. I apologized, and I know it was wrong, but everyone is saying that I said something completely different. Miranda and her friends twisted my words. What I said was wrong, I know, but if you're going to post how bad of a person I am all over social media, at least get your shit right.

This chick named Rei, thought that making a Facebook post about me would solve all of the problems. Only, she called me pathetic for making fun of someone for being pregnant, even though they aren't. I never said Miranda was pregnant, and I never would ever make fun of someone who was pregnant.

I know how easily accidents can happen, and I don't think someone should be shamed for that. Yet, they said that I make fun of everyone who is pregnant. Bull crap. I would never make fun of someone for that. Never, ever, ever. Stuff like that happens, and people don't want it to most likely in high school, and chances are they're scared out of their freaking mind, and being judged will be one of the first things on their mind. I seriously would never make fun of someone for that.

I can't imagine how scary that would be. Having to tell your partner, parents, and friends at such a young age. That would scare me shitless, to be honest with you. I would probably rather kill myself over having to tell my parents that I was pregnant. I'm not kidding either. In my mind, that's the most scary thing ever, so I wouldn't make fun of someone else for that.

But, you know how fast rumors spread. So, word on the street is that I am making fun of people for being pregnant, even though none of them are. Seriously? The messed up part is that people believe it. I guess nobody really knows me, but still, I know I would never do that.

People get pregnant in high school. Accidents happen. I couldn't imagine how scary it is. Honestly, it's probably my biggest fear aside from losing certain family and friends. I would never, ever make up a rumor about someone, especially if it were about being pregnant. Let's just get that out of the way. Never in a million years would I make up a lie that someone is pregnant. Got it? Good.

So, people are posting about me. Rei is the one who started it all. She thinks that calling me a bad person, a bully, pathetic, solves everything when it doesn't. Here's some advice for you guys. If someone does something wrong, and you feel the need to change it, confront them first. I can see certain situations where calling someone out is appropriate, but this one is just weird. If I were to be calling Miranda pregnant and being as mean as they said I was, call me a bad person and post about it. If I didn't apologize, and didn't see anything wrong with it, do it. But you see, this isn't the case. I'm not exactly mad that they're posting about my wrongdoings, it's that they are posting lies about me.

First off, it is the first time that it has has happened. I don't find it necessary to post constantly calling me such a terrible person, but I guess I deserve it. Like I said before, it's that they're making up this false story. If you really want changed behavior from said person, talk to them. If you're posting it on social media to cause more drama, and you keep going and going and making up lies, you really don't care about the wrongdoings, because you aren't trying to put the situation to rest one-on-one.

The first post didn't really bother me until people started commenting on it. This one chick named Krista, was saying that I'm "Out of control." Okay, I don't get that. The definition of out of control is: no longer possible to manage. What the heck?

So, let's see, everyone's posting on social media on how bad of a person I am, but guess how many confronted me? None. They all sat behind a screen and laughed at me in comment sections. As if that would do anything. Silly girls. None of them messaged me, but they did in fact feel it necessary to update it all to social media. Alright, do that I guess. But at least try and talk to me. I really did feel bad, but they wouldn't let me show them. Whenever I'd message one of them and try to explain my side, the told me to leave them alone.

They continued to post stuff, and it was really bringing me down. Mostly when everyone was calling me a bad person. It's the only thing that I'm holding onto. I got pushed back a lot from those words. Sure, they didn't call me fat, like I called Miranda, but it hurt. I probably deserved it, but it's the worst thing that you can say to me. It really is.

My sister doesn't know it, but every time she calls me Ms. Suicide, or makes fun of my mental health issues, it hurts me, so bad. I can't control it. I'm so sick of people thinking that I chose this life. I don't choose to be like this. I want to be healthy more than anything. Really, I do. I want my life back.

But if I didn't have depression and anxiety, I wouldn't have written this book. I wouldn't have talked all of those people out of suicide. I wouldn't be helping people. Sure, it sucks having it. I'm just glad I get to understand it and help others through it. So, for people to make fun of me for it, or to tell me to stop, it hurts. I can't stop. It offends me. It really does.

The next day, I didn't go to school. It wasn't because of them, it was because I had pneumonia and I was sick as poop. My boyfriend texts me and tells me he might be getting arrested. Well, what they heck? I have no idea what he could have done. I was getting really worried. I texted him back right away, but he never answered.

I started over thinking like crazy. I didn't know what he could have done, and him not answering, worried me even more. After several minutes of racing thoughts, my phone lit up. "Luke is typing…" Snapchat told me. That took

another couple minutes and what he said
next, shocked me.

XLVI

Apparently, Miranda told the cops that Luke sexually assaulted her when we went to McDonald's. Bull crap! I found that complete bull. For one, she was at work. He was in the drive thru, how would he sexually assault her there? Secondly, why would he do anything sexual with his ex, in front of his girlfriend and her little sister? Miranda, well, getting me in trouble is one thing, because I deserved it, but getting my boyfriend in trouble is another.

I was furious. I didn't know who to talk to. I can't talk to my counselor anymore. I found out that she has been telling the principal everything that I say. Now, she is a mandated reporter. She has to report certain things, but what she told wasn't under what she has to say to me. So, I lost all trust for her. Still, I wouldn't let this just happen. Luke did nothing wrong, Miranda just wants him in jail. She even told me this. She saw an an opportunity and struck. She wanted this.

So, I decided to email my guidance counselor because I'm not going to let it get this far.

"I know what I did was wrong. I've apologized on multiple occasions. I've tried so hard for them to understand that I'm sorry, and I know what I did was wrong. I've apologized to so many people. They keep twisting the story, though. They keep saying I'm calling her pregnant because I'm jealous of her. I never called her pregnant. That's the thing. It's just getting out of hand now.

For starters, Miranda is now saying that Luke sexually assaulted her. That's the biggest bucket of bull crap that I've ever heard in my life. Not just me, but my sister was also with when he supposedly 'assaulted her.' Watch the cameras there, listen to the conversation because I can guarantee that nothing even close to being sexual was said or done. He had nothing to do with this situation, Miranda is just the type of person who gets joy out of seeing others suffer. I'm not like that, so I felt terrible when I heard that she got upset over it. Of course, I didn't think about it when I did it - which is stupid of me - but she does that kind of stuff intentionally. So please, if anyone should get in trouble, it's me, not Luke. He did absolutely nothing. But now they're all just posting things on social media and what they're saying is ridiculous. For one, they're completely changing my words. For two, they're posting on how I'm a "bully." Okay so, to be a bully, it's continuous and intentional hurting someone either physically or emotionally.

I made a joke. Yes, I really do understand that it was wrong, I understand that it was wrong. But I'm not a fan of hers for sleeping with my boyfriend when she had a boyfriend of her own. - I know that it still doesn't make it okay, - but everyone is now spreading stupid rumors about me being "out of control." They're saying I'm full of crap because I say I'm depressed, yet I'm mean to everyone.

I honestly have saved so many lives, and everyone is telling me I'm a bad person over one mistake I made? I was wrong and I am so sorry. I've apologized. The best apology is changed action, and if the people would stop attacking me for 5 minutes, they would see that I'm not like that. I must've just wanted to get a laugh over it. I wanted to feel good because I haven't in so long.

I thought that putting her down in my mind would boost me up, and in that moment it did. I just didn't think about it.

Everyone now thinks I'm a bad person... But I'm not. I know that I'm not. That's the only thing that I'm holding onto... Is me being a good person. I just want them to stop being mean. I want them to understand that I'm sorry."

"I also agree that you have a good heart and that this one incident is not who you are!! I was hoping to calm the whole thing down when I met with you, but could tell it hit a nerve in you. Now, I understand what that nerve was. There was way more to this story then I had any idea. I think if you can give it time, people will move on and so can you, it just takes time and healing on both ends.

I am sorry that you have lost some trust in me and there are times I have to share things with Heather as my principal (but there are not many)! When a student walks out of my room and I am scared for them, I will tell as many people as I can to keep them safe. Including my principal, their parent, and even their friends and the nurse. My job is challenging in what things I must keep confidential and what things must be reported for welfare concerns and helping others. I am sorry that this situation caused you so much hurt and also others.

You are not a bully and I would go on record in saying that as well, you made a poor decision and I believe you have now owned that!

Mrs. W"

She wasn't taking action, I had to do something else. Well, she had some good advice. I just waited it out. It started to slow down, so that's good. Luke's dad ended up coming into the school and raising hell. I think that's funny. Luke's dad is awesome.

So, Luke ended up off the hook. I was so happy to hear that. And as of right now, I'm just letting everything sizzle down. I don't want anything to do with drama. This is why I'm not friends with a lot of girls. I'm not putting a stereotype on all girls, I know there's a lot like me, who hate drama. But most that I know, it's their entire life. Drama. I hate it so much. Well, all that I can do is just wait it out. So, that's just what I am doing. Waiting it out.

XLVII

Guys, it's been just over six months that I've decided to start writing a book. That's pretty cool, isn't it? I'm so proud of myself. Right now, as of October 17th, 2016, I am very happy with where life is. I'm hoping it lasts a little longer than usual this time.

The thing with Miranda slowed down, Luke and I are doing pretty good. I mean, he's convinced me to take my antidepressants every day so our relationship gets better. I really hope he and I last. He means the entire world to me. Anyways, you already know about that.

So, depending on whether or not you liked this book, I am going to be finishing it soon. How many authors tell their reader that they're almost done? Haha, I don't know. But, this book has helped me through so much. I can't believe that it started out at as argumentative essay. Look how far I've gotten. I went from a girl who felt that she was worthless, to a 14 year old - well, I'll be 15 in like two weeks - who is already saving lives. I wrote a book for goodness sake.

I'm already set on my future. I want to help people, and I am already taking steps towards my goals. I am proud of myself. I really am. Just think about how bad I was. I didn't know anything about myself that was good. Seriously, I thought that I was a waste of space. All that I saw myself as was a screwup. I had a messed up head. I didn't do anything productive in my life. I had zero accomplishments.

I couldn't do anything that I set my mind to. I had people all around me saying how amazing I was, but I didn't see it. I never could.

When I was younger, I never thought that bad about myself. I had really good confidence. I look back at pictures and you can see, I really didn't care about how people saw me. My hair was a complete mess and my clothes didn't match all of the time. But there I was with the biggest smile on my face. I didn't care about what anyone thought of me because I thought that I was a pretty cool little girl.

I was always making people laugh and smile, but I didn't really treat people right. I don't think that I was a very good person. But that's how a lot of people still are. Maybe it's just a trait of being immature. I was

very immature, and I still can be. I've
still learned a lot. I've learned so
much. I've grown so much, it's
unbelievable. At least I see it, and
you as the reader can probably pick it
out, too.

I've gotten better. Of course,
it's not perfect, but it's life. There
are going to be ups and downs. It isn't
always going to be sunshine. I know
that. But at least it isn't always
storming anymore. I've learned that
even in the bad situations, there are
good things. It's really hard to look
at things this way though.

For example, look at me. Life was
so hard for a long time but now, well,
it still is. But if I wouldn't have
gone through those tough times, I
wouldn't be writing this. I'd still be

a bitch to everyone. I'm glad that I'm not that person anymore.

It's never too late to change. Be the kind of person you wish to see more of in this world. If someone looks nice, tell them. A compliment goes a long way. These little things that I've been told my whole life, they are actually the big things. They build character. Not only does it make them feel better about themselves, but it makes you as well. It's beautiful, isn't it? I sure think so. Hit two birds with one stone. I guess that isn't the best word choice.

Anyways, for the past three weeks, I knew what I was going to end my book with. I was certain, it would be perfect. Let's start back to September 23. It was just an average day. I got up, trudged on through the day and that's that. I was sitting in my least favorite class, and for some reason, I decided to take my phone with me. I usually just keep it in my locker because there's no signal in the school anyways. I had a weird feeling that I should take it with me.

After countless worksheets, my phone rang. It was on vibrate but it startled me. Now, it really shouldn't have been different. I always get random calls. I usually answer them because a lot of times it's someone reaching out for help. My teacher would have flipped out if she saw me on my phone.

I let it ring, as the want to know ate me alive. Who could it be? What if someone needs help? I took my phone out of my pocket and slid it over. It was too late, I missed the call.

By this time the teacher was walking over to me so I shoved my phone into my pocket and sat back down. I didn't need to get in trouble again. There was just something about that call. I couldn't explain it, and I still can't, but I should have answered it.

I continue to do my work (Haha! Good one. Me, do my work? I bet you guys didn't believe that one.) I dazed off and entered my own world. I'm a lot better than I was a year ago. A year ago, my thoughts would have been eating me alive. Dazing off would be the worst possible thing for me. But, I'm getting better, and the bad thoughts come less. It was safe to think again.

Finally. The bell rings, and I continue the same process. After sitting in class and waiting, the bell rings to get out of hell. Yay. I go home. As my mom pulls into the driveway, the thought of that phone calls enters my cloudy mind again.

I take out my phone, and click on the red numbers. It starts ringing. My mind raced with questions. Moments later, no answer. Oh well, it was probably just a scam anyways. I go inside, drop off my bags and run out to the four-wheeler to clear my mind. As I'm cruising away, I have to pee.

I go inside and see that I had a missed call from that number, plus a voicemail. Weird. I do my business, and go back outside. Going on my four-wheeler seems to be the only thing that clears my mind nowadays. It was a couple hours later and I decided to just chill at home.

My boyfriend wasn't there, and everyone was preoccupied. I grabbed a plastic baggy and went over to the a closet in our hallway. I started opening pill bottles and dropping various pills inside of the bag. There were so many, and I knew these all would kill me. I've started being able to recognize pills and their purposes.

With the bag of my future, I walked into my room and hid them in a pocket of one of my old jackets. I had a plan. I went to sleep. Once I woke, I opened my eyes up to my boyfriend laying next to me. He knew that I was having a rough day at school the day before, so he came over that morning to cheer me up. I was still sleeping, but oh well.

I woke up and hugged him. He said he had to go ask my mom something, so he ran upstairs. The same thing happened as before. The thought of that call and voicemail, crowded my head again. I jumped up, grabbed my phone and laid in my bed.

When the words sunk into my head, I screamed and ran upstairs to tell my mother the life changing news. I felt like I was going to cry, everything felt as if it were in slow motion as my feet pitter pattered up the stairs. My mom heard nothing as she was outside, I opened the door, and told her to shush, and played the voicemail.

It was hard to hear, but as soon as she heard it, her face lit up almost as much as mine did. It was from a guy from the Vikings! I jumped up and down and it looked like my mom was going to cry.

I didn't really know what to expect. It mentioned Blair Walsh and the letter I wrote him this summer, but it didn't go into detail. What if he wanted to meet me? Oh my gosh! So, yeah I was super happy jumping up and down.

I tried to call the guy back but there wasn't an answer. My mom said he probably wouldn't pick up on the weekend. I had to wait until Monday to find out what was going on. The thought of suicide wasn't even on my mind. Isn't that something? I spent those couple of days screaming at my mom to check her email every five seconds.

Then Monday came around. It was also homecoming week so the dress up day was pajama day. My favorite. I had to explain to my teachers that I had to leave my volume up on my phone because I was expecting a very important phone call. They didn't really care so that was great. I waited.

At third hour it was hallway decorating time. I wondered why I didn't get a call back. I walked down to my mom's office to ask her if she got an email from him. She said no, and I asked her if I should just call him. I figured she'd say no, but she said sure.

Oh gosh. I got so nervous. I could barely take my phone out of my pocket. My armpits were fricken moist as hell and I was shaking. No, not now come on. I finally had the bravery to dial the numbers. I kept saying, "Hi, Brandon, this is Camryn," over and over in my head.

Finally, there was an answer. Our conversation changed my perspective on life for that short while. I can 100%

guarantee that I have never, ever been so happy in my entire life.

I was informed that they read my pep-talk letter to Blair, and he said it was a very powerful letter and he wanted to meet me. I was so freaking happy. My mom took a video of my reaction and it was priceless. You could just see my eyes light up. It was amazing. I was about to cry. My face was red and my smile was enormous.

After the conversation, I had to go back to class. Everyone was shocked to see me so happy. I've never smiled like that before. My smile must have been contagious, because once someone looked at me, they smiled, too. It was simply amazing. It didn't take long to see everyone smiling. My classmates were truly happy for me. Everyone looked happy, and it was just a magical moment. Everyone knows how much I love Blair Walsh, and for me to finally get to meet him was just extraordinary.

As soon as I put my head down, I was crying. I was crying because I was so freaking happy. Everyone started making fun of me, but we were all smiling. It was just amazing.

I had to leave class because I was crying, so I went into the bathroom and smiled while I was crying. I was just so happy I kept telling myself, "Blair Walsh wants to meet you!" It was the most amazing feeling in the world. Suicide was the last thing on my mind. Why would I want to die if the most amazing thing to ever happen in my life is going to happen? I couldn't. I had to live to see Blair Walsh.

Throughout the days, I was constantly telling my mom to check her email. I was very suicidal, but whenever I'd reach for the bag of pills I would think about getting to meet Blair Walsh. Wow, I'd be dead if it weren't for him. I wanted to die a lot. I was very seriously thinking about it, but honestly, I was not going to pass up my chance to meet my favorite person. That would be a stupid move, and I wouldn't do it. No matter how bad I just wanted to give up, I couldn't. I was going to live. I had to.

XLVIII

The guy finally emailed my mom
back and apologized about taking so
long. When I found out the date and
stuff, I don't know. I didn't jump up
in excitement or start crying like last
time. It just didn't feel real. I still
told myself that I had to live, I had
to. I wanted to die so bad though.

Let's see, the Miranda shit that I
told you about, well, Luke got out of
his pickle. I was very happy about
that. But then, that girls boyfriend
emailed my mom (a part time teacher)
and threatened her. He said that we
tried to run both of them off of the
road. I have no idea where that came
from. He said that I told the principal
that Miranda was calling me names.
Then, he closed his statement by

calling me "suicidal." That was a whole shit ton of crap, and her family tried to get the police involved, but it was quickly proven that it wasn't true. Nothing happened to the two lying scumbags though. I don't talk to either of them or even look at them. They're just trying to start drama. It slowed down again.

I lost my best friend, too. You guys know that. He left me. We still aren't talking and it hurts. It really does. Sometimes I'll text him and ask him how his day was. You know, just to check up on him because I still really care about him. He never shows interest anymore though. So, I quickly stop talking and he carries on just fine without me. Why did I think differently? I don't know. It sure hurts, I can tell you that. But yeah, I was really down.

My parents want to get back together, and I know that's what I wanted at first, but I don't know anymore. I don't think it's a good idea. Life has just been rough. Luke and I have been doing okay, too. I'm not close with anyone anymore.

After waiting to meet my role model, the day fast approached. I got to meet Blair Walsh. It was very, very awkward. When I walked in and saw him, I thought for sure that I was going to cry. He was short and had amazing hair. His teeth were seriously the whitest thing that I've ever seen in my life, and his eyes were just like mine. I've always hated my eyes, but they looked great on him.

He greeted me with a smile and a handshake. I stood there like a deer in the headlights. I had the cheesiest smile across my face. I really wanted a hug. We walked into the room that they practice in and it was huge.

We talked a bit but it was pretty awkward. He asked me if I had any questions. Boy, I had a ton. This is my role model that we are talking about. I wanted to know everything. My mind was blank. I organized so many questions to ask him. All that came to mind was, "What's your favorite color?" Stupid. Wow, I'm stupid. At least I know that his favorite color is red and black. Mine is neon blue and black. Blair actually hates the color purple, that's pretty ironic, isn't it? I was so embarrassed.

I could tell that he didn't want to be there. I could tell my presence didn't really mean much to him at all. It hurt really bad. But, I have to suck it up. I mean, I AM MEETING MY FAVORITE NFL PLAYER OF ALL TIMES! I was happy.

After 20 minutes, our time together was over. We took pictures, I raced my sister, I convinced him to make a dubsmash with me. Heck, he even said he would shave his beard for me. Overall, it was an absolutely amazing experience.

XLIX

So, you've followed me on this emotional roller coaster for six months. You've read so many situations, emotions, and you - with or without depression - have connected to many of the thoughts that I am experiencing on a daily basis.

The truth is, everyone experiences this stuff. Everyone goes through a point in their life where they're depressed. Yes, there's definitely a big difference in a rough time and a mental health disorder, but the truth is, life sucks butt. Everyone has to go through the poopy days.

But I learned to look at things differently. Look around you. The world is seriously so beautiful. The colors, the running water, the way people's smiles fold; it's all so many reasons to stop and think about how beautiful life really is. I look at the little things.

These six months that I have been writing, I completely changed my mindset. I am not a bad person anymore. I'm not at all. I am honestly so proud of myself. I am so glad that I am alive. What? Did the suicidal girl seriously just say she is happy that she's alive? Oh my gosh, what's happening here?

Well, in the very, very long lasting process, I learned to love myself. I am beautiful. I don't look in the mirror and go straight to that giant pimple on my nose anymore. I don't go to my messed up hair in the morning or my godawful breath before I brush my teeth. Instead, I go the my smile, or my green eyes. I don't look down at my belly and say I'm over weight, I look at my butt and say, "Damn, those squats are paying off. Go Camryn." You see, it sounds easy, doesn't it? Trust me, it's not. You can't just chose to think you're beautiful. You can't.

I went from hating every little thing about me to loving myself. I'm glad that I'm me. I am very talented. Look at me, I'm writing a book. I'm so set on helping people, I know what I want to do when I get older. I've saved so many lives and that's absolutely amazing. I should be proud of myself, shouldn't I? This is the first time I've ever admitted such nice things to myself… It's a different feeling.

Why was I so hard on myself before? I had the mindset that I'm a screwup, but I really am not. I've had the mindset that at 14 years old, I accomplished nothing. I changed that. Look at me, reaching my dreams and goals. I'm not worthless. I will get through this. I will continue to accomplish things in life.

I understand now that there are highs and lows in life. Like I mentioned before, this entire book was just lows, lows, lows. In my life, it really wasn't just lows, it just seemed like it. The big things, involved this book. Reaching 10 pages, then 50, then 100, then 200, it was amazing for me. I felt like I was accomplishing so much, because I was and will continue to.

A year ago, everyone said, "It will get better. Give it time, be patient." I've learned that isn't true. I always thought that it was impossible for me to get better, and if I just waited, nothing would happen. You can't just sit back and watch things be good again. What sense does that make?

Instead, you have to work for things. You hear it all the time, but it's so true. One of my favorite quotes are, "The goal isn't to live forever, it's to create something that will." I love it. I want to do just that. So, these past couple months I've really been working towards getting better. No cutting, no suicide attempts, just try to stay positive.

L

Hello

This gap was about a four month difference. Wow. It's been a while. Well, I honestly don't even know where to start.

I'll start with an update on Luke and I. I broke up with him. Shocking, right? I couldn't live without him, he was my world, so what happened? It's true. I thought that I was going to marry him. I thought that we would buy our own house together, and have kids someday. I would have given anything for his happiness, and that was the problem. I let him treat me like shit for far too long, 16 months to be exact. Him and I were together for 16 months, and we looked like the happiest couple ever. All my posts on instagram well, you could see the smiles plastered across our faces. You could just see how much I loved him by the way I looked at him. It wasn't exactly a lie, he made me happy. He made me smile, and there were lots of times he made me happy to be alive. But, I had to be honest with myself. Was there more times he made me want to live, or die? I mean, he cheated on me with several people. Not just Holly and Miranda, many more. Several months of relationships with other girls, one night stands, while he was still with me. He lied all of the time and constantly seemed to be putting me down or underestimating me. I've always known in my gut that he was no good for me, I always knew I didn't deserve what I got from him, but I loved him, and his happiness was my top priority. I always felt it in my gut that I should leave, but I couldn't. It hurt not to have him being mine. It hurt to think of him with another girl. But, in all honesty, I was in love with a fake relationship. I was in love with the idea of being happy with someone, and I ignored the fact that he put me through hell, and I called it love. I liked taking cute pictures together, and having everyone say we were the cutest couple ever. But what they didn't know, was my nicely done makeup in our homecoming picture had to be redone about four times, and just moments before that cute picture of us kissing, we were calling each other names. We looked in love and happy, but that was not love, and I feel like I've always known it in the back of my head. I always said, "I know," whenever someone would tell me that I should leave, I always agreed that I didn't deserve to be put through what I did, but I stayed because it hurt not having him there. But I am strong, I know I'm strong, and I can live without him. I will not keep going back to what keeps destroying me.

My bunny Charlie died. She was on my agenda to write about, but I never really did. I've mentioned Rilee before, and I was going to write about a specific day with him. During the summer, I hung out with him at the fair, and made the decision to get a bunny. She was literally the cutest thing I've ever seen.

She died in my arms. I went to get a pop from the garage and decided to call for her. I didn't check on her all day. I was in bed all day. I was super sick. "Char Char!" I'd call enthusiastically. Her happy self didn't run up and greet me, so I peered into her cage. She looked sick, and I suddenly could feel hot tears forming in my eyes.

I called mom crying and told her she was dying, then I just held her. She wouldn't eat or drink, or even move. She kept falling over, so I just held her. I cried the hardest I believe I ever cried in my life. I begged for her not to leave me. I kept telling her how much I loved her, and when I let go, she flipped over and her body went straight and she died.

I screamed so loud. Once that first tear rolled down my cheek after I knew she was dead, everything broke free. She left me. In the last six months, she's helped me a lot for not even being able to talk.

When I first saw her, I sent my mom a picture of her. Well, $15 later, she was mine. My mom wasn't too happy when I brought home a bunny from the fair. She was too cute to pass up. Later that day, I spent $100 buying a cage, and the rest of the bunny supplies needed. I felt like a somebody with her. What I mean by that is, well, first, she learned her name. Then, she learned "come here Charlie," then she learned how to dance which was just running in circles, and then she learned how to give kisses. I was doing something with my life. Something small, but I was doing something. I felt like I had worth.

After a while, Charlie was able to pick up on my emotions. If I was anxious, she would hide. If I was upset, she would cuddle with me, or if I were crying, she would lick the tears off of my face.

She was a smart pain in the butt. Charlie was a psycho. She got high off of Smarties once. She's been through more than most bunnies. She got to travel to school with me and meet a lot of people. She's gotten to ride four-wheeler with me. She even got to go on the trampoline. She's outsmarted several dogs that have tried to attack her.

I'll always miss you, Charles the transgender bunny. You've helped me more than friends that I have. Sounds weird, but she meant a lot to me. I love you Charlie. Rest In Peace. That hit me hard. She was beautiful and perfect. I miss her.

What's next? Well, I also found out that I am bipolar which explains a lot. I scored 100% on the test, and I didn't believe it. So, I had to do it again, but I got the same. My pills work for Bipolar II disorder, too. That's really, really bad when I don't take my pills. I almost got my mom fired too. That's a long story and I'll save it for later.

December 23, I was having a rough day. We went shopping for Christmas and I spent hundreds of dollars on my mom, Luke, Violet and Ricky. Luke said some girl was hot so I was really upset. Note, this is when we were still together. I was quiet in the car. You can probably imagine what I was thinking about. I kept my mouth shut and just chilled once I got home. I was obviously bummed. My thoughts were eating me alive.

All of a sudden, my mom calls for me. I walk up the stairs to be greeted by my mom with something under her jacket. I was weirded out. I knew something was up when saw Violet recording. Under her jacket, was an adorable puppy. If you guys have ever stalked me on social media, you would know that I'm obsessed with dogs. I have two already named Bella and Maddie. Bella is seven and she's a Yorkie. Maddie is almost four, and she's a chocolate lab. I love dogs so much. I honestly wish people were more like dogs.

Seth is still gone. I don't miss him as much as I did a few months ago. I know now that he just filled me with lies. I really never meant anything to him. It hurt to go through such a loss, but everything happens for a reason, you know? I don't need anyone that doesn't need me. I still always smile when I see him smile. I'm glad that he's happy with his girlfriend. She's so beautiful. He got lucky. It's been very hard without having him by my side. I have been going through so much by myself, but it's making me stronger.

My teachers and principal are still the same. Well, actually, a few of my teachers have really been looking out for me and that makes me happy, My principal actually just said that depression isn't that bad to one of my new friends, Kaitlyn. Kaitlyn is new to this school, but she is constantly getting bullied by her "friends." Remind you of anything?

I'm doing my best to help her. We are actually becoming really good friends. We talk to each other about a lot and it feels really good to have a friend. She has been there for me this past month, and I'm so grateful to have her in my life.

Most of the girls in my grade don't know how to be friends. They would throw their best friend under the bus, as long as it benefited them. I haven't had a real friend in such a long time. I can honestly say that she is my best friend. I was crying one night, and she drove all the way to my house to give me McDonald's and stay the night with me. We ended up skipping school the next day and just hanging out. It was much needed for both of us. People were being so mean to her.

Remember how much I hate the principal at my school? Well, I tried to get her fired. That didn't go too well. I made an online petition, and it kinda got a bunch of attention. So many of even the "good" kids, wrote about their experiences with our terrible principal. It didn't just happen to me, it happened to almost everyone.

My principal told other students that their mental health wasn't important to her also. I wasn't the only one, and that spoke a lot. I really wanted to change things when I saw how much she affected other people's lives in negative way, as well. Putting people down when they're going through a tough time is the absolute worst thing that you can do. So, I made the petition.

First, I actually emailed the school board president, and he never answered, but he did forward it to my principal and superintendent. That's when everything went wrong. Now, they didn't talk to me. They talked to my mom. They didn't take any concern in anyone else's experiences, let alone mine. They called her down to tell her that it needed to be taken down and blah blah. They called her in there to threaten her job, as a part time teacher.

You know how little money my family makes in the first place, so for my mom to lose her job would be the most terrible thing that could happen. My mom kept pestering me to take it down but I wouldn't. I am not going to let people continue to be treated like this. Plus, they couldn't fire my mom for my doings, could they?

The people with power are a lot more sinister than my 15 year old mind thought. My mom explained that they could easily make something up that would look like a legal reason to fire her to everyone else. My mom was a bigger priority so, I had to take it down.

I had to talk with the superintendent, and I lost my computer for a long time so I couldn't write at all. That's another reason that I couldn't write, and another reason I failed two classes. School rocks, man.

Why else have I been gone for so long? Well, I've been so stressed out. I don't know the next step. I've been searching for publishers left and right, but I can't find one that fits me. If I'd find one that would like to have books on mental health, they didn't want any biographies or autobiographies. Technically, my book falls under the category of being an autobiography since I'm telling you my story.

Man, oh man, this isn't easy at all. This has been the most stressful, and difficult challenge that has ever been thrown at me. Giving up? Yeah, I was sure of it. These past couple of months, becoming an offical author wasn't in my future. I had given up.

I've tried to go through other routes, too. Traditional publishing wasn't going to work, so maybe I could go with self publishing. After days of research, I came to realize that this couldn't be an option. My family doesn't have the extra cash laying around needed to self publish a book. Man, it's expensive. We can barely afford groceries, never the less having extra thousands of dollars hanging out of my back pocket. Giving up seemed to be the only option.

Once I officially announced that I can no longer go through with publishing my book, everyone blew up telling me that I cannot give up. They didn't understand why though. After explaining and wishing that money didn't rule the world, people finally started to understand. Many people suggested making a GoFundMe, but I thought that it would be selfish to ask for money from other people. I was stuck in a rut.

After lots of convincing from my supporters, I finally put up a GoFundMe. I mean this book was written to help people, that's the opposite of selfish. I think I recieved donations for about four days, and then nothing. Although it wasn't popular, it did give me some hope. I raised a decent amount of money. I was set on continuing to finish my book.

Now, this obviously didn't take place over the entire four month period of not writing. What else set me back? I still didn't have enough money, so I didn't even think about touching my book.

So, writing is my go-to for when I'm sad, right? So you can only imagine what a mess I was. I took about a four month break. It was absolutely terrible. When I was writing, I didn't have a care in the world. Writing is a better antidepressant than any pill you could ever give me.

I was a complete monster to be honest. It was like someone came up and sucked all of my views and beliefs out of me. I felt like I was a bad person again. I wasn't me. It's hard to explain. I didn't seem to care about the wellbeing of myself, let alone others. I was everything that I hate in people; I was a bad person. I mean, I guess I wasn't mean to people, I just didn't care. I didn't compliment people every time that I thought someone looked beautiful or when their haircut looked nice. I didn't care. I knew that wasn't me. So, here I am, writing.

I am complete when I write. I remember who I am and what I am supposed to be doing. Like I said, it's my antidepressant. With my pills, sure, I'm alright. But when I write, I'm equal. I'm who I am supposed to be.

This whole time I was writing to save other people's lives, but I was also saving mine. Writing is the reason my perspective got flipped around. It's the reason that every whisper I hear in the halls, doesn't make my mind think it's about me, but if it is, it's their problem.

LI

Something not important

"Stop it!" I screamed with everything that I had. He forced his lips onto my mine. I will admit, that I felt at home for the first time in weeks. I fell into the trap. I was scared. *What if he hits me? What do I do?* My mind was blank. I didn't fight him away. I didn't really move. I stayed quiet.

"We can't do this. We can't kiss if we aren't together anymore."
That didn't stop him. He kept going and going no matter what I said. He picked me up and put me on top of the trunk of his crappy car. He pushed my arms behind my head and laid on top of me. *This cannot be happening. What do I do?*

"Stop. I don't want this."

"Baby, I want you to be mine again."

Those words alone made my heart hurt a little less. I felt less edgy. I felt a little bit better. All of the emotions that were built up inside of me subsided. Just those stupid words, made everything feel okay, That's the problem. I don't want him to mean so much to me. I don't want to have to look for his face in a crowded room anymore. I don't want to love him anymore. Those words caught me off guard. I saw his hands holding another girl's, and his smile was directed towards every girl that walked by. He got to go to parties, and have sex with all of the other seniors in his class. He got to get high every night with his friends. He was free, and happy, and I was alone and missing him. He was out drinking and kissing the group of girls he told me that he would never talk to because they're all drama, while I was in my room crying over the thought of him not being mine. It's funny how life works. I didn't eat. I just couldn't. I couldn't sleep. My mind was constantly filled with, *what if's*. My mind was always thinking of the way his eyebrows moved when I'd make him smile. My mind would think about all of the times that we would talk about our future. The dogs we would get. The names of our future kids. The type of house we wanted and even the location. I could finally see my future thanks to him. I could finally say that I knew a perfect person. My definition of perfect isn't excluding flaws, it's loving them. I love everything about him. I love his laugh that he hated and how he needed "one more kiss" eight more times before he could leave. I love how we could do anything and still be having fun. I love how we both tried new things together. I love how amazing he was. I love how much he tried. It isn't just this. I still loved his morning breath and nasty ass farts. I still loved it when he's so mad he wants to punch everyone he sees. I still loved him when he called me a cunt and a whore, and told me that my problems were, and I quote, "Stupid fucking bullshit." I still loved him when he left, and cheated and lied. I still loved him when he gave me a bloody nose. I still loved him when he shoved me up against the wall and I still loved him when he forced me to do things that I didn't want to do. I still love him. I love everything about him, but I still had some respect for myself. Now, I know better than to just let him take advantage of me. I know that he would just leave right away. He just wanted to use me. I knew that. If he wanted me, he would show it. If he wanted me, he would have texted me or called me. If he wanted me, he would prove it. If he wanted to date me, he wouldn't do this. So, I told him no. But that didn't stop him. His words soaked into my mind and left a permanent imprint, whereas mine bounced right off of his. I kissed him back. I need this. I ran my fingers through his hair. I missed him. I missed his lips. He pulled my pants off of my body and I jumped to my feet and pulled them up.

"You are just using me."

"No, I want you to be mine."

He pulled my pants back down and pushed me to the side of his car. His cold hands grabbed my face and pulled me closer. He put his tongue in my mouth. His breathing got heavy. His hands were moving across my body. I was pressed against his freezing car. My mind was as frozen as my body. *What do I do?*

"Do you want me?" He whispered in my ear.

I didn't respond. I was too scared. He started touching me. I was paralyzed. I couldn't move. He pushed me down and unzipped his pants. He kept forcing my head towards his body.

"Come on. I know you want to." Moments later I stood up and he pushed me into his car, again, kissing me. He opened his car door and shoved me onto the seats. My mind was blank. It wasn't flooding with thoughts like before, it was numb. He put all of his weight on top of me. I didn't say a word. I didn't scream. I didn't fight him. I didn't do anything but lay there. I didn't want it to happen, it just did. I don't want to say that I let it happen because I didn't. He was stronger than me. I couldn't get away. No one would hear me if I screamed, and I don't think that I could build up the courage to do it in the first place. And just as fast as it started, it ended.

I walked inside. My body was still frozen, as was my mind. First, I went to the bathroom. It was running down my leg. Next, I walked downstairs, and sat in my bed. *I can't tell anyone this. No one will believe me. Everyone will think that I'm one of those girls that had sex with their boyfriend and turned*

them in after they broke up for
revenge. No one will believe me. I
covered up and thought very hard on
what to do. Let's just say that I
didn't get much sleep that night.

LII

The next day at school he avoided me. I was scared. I know how easily these things can be switched around. I could be called a slut, or maybe even a cunt. He could tell people the opposite of what actually happened. Maybe I came onto him. Who knows what could happen? I was a teenage girl in highschool. Anything is possible. I felt like I was carrying the weight of the world on my shoulders, and I really needed to let it out. So, I talked to one of my good friends Emily. We both confide in each other a lot, and I trust her very much. She told me that I needed to turn him in. I really didn't want to. "Please don't tell anyone." When the thought of the same thing happening to another girl entered my thought process, I immediately changed my mind. So, I asked if I could go talk to the counselor. I knew if I told her she would have to report it, so when I arrived, I told her that something very bad happened, but I can't tell her because she would have to tell. She thought for a moment and asked what it had to do with. I said rape. She looked shocked. I felt embarrassment flush throughout my body. *This is my fault. What am I doing? Why am I here? Telling will just make him even worse. I don't want to ruin his life either. I love him. I don't want to see him get nowhere in life. What should I do?* She asked me if the said person who was raped was over 18, and I said no. She thought for a moment again.

"Is the other person over 18?"

"Yes."

Without giving any details, I was able to at least let it out. I wanted to talk to my other teacher because I trust him more than anyone else in the world. That's right, a good teacher. So many teachers treat their students like shit, but I am so happy and appreciative that there is one that's different at my school. I emailed him and said, "Something very, very bad happened." We set up a time to meet, and I already felt better. I had a lot on my mind. When the time came, I told him the same thing that I told my counselor. I had my ex in class during that period of time, so I was killing two birds with one stone. I wanted to just let everything out, but I'm always a bottle and I never take off my lid. I told him that the counselor didn't need to report the situation because I didn't give her information, and that made me feel a lot better. So, he told me to word it like I did with her so that he didn't necessarily have to - unless he felt as if I were in danger. Once I said, "rape," his face went pale and he couldn't even look at me. I wondered if this was a mistake. I wondered if I should have just kept this to myself. *It is my fault. I could have avoided this.* He wasn't disappointed in me. He didn't blame me. I felt bad and embarrassed. *I ruined his day. Now he probably hates me, or thinks I'm crazy.* I folded the sleeves of my shirt and twisted them. I looked down onto the floor and sat in silence. I wanted to get up and walk away. I wanted to cry, or scream. I wanted to disappear. I didn't want to make him mad or sad, but I'm pretty sure that I did. When I looked up, he spoke. It wasn't discouraging, or mean. He felt bad for me. He didn't ask very many questions at all, but I wish he did. I wanted to talk about it with someone. I don't have anyone to talk to. I trust him. I need to talk to him. Instead of saying anything, I listened, which also helps. It kind of fuels to the fire inside my head, but it also helps. Even though it gets my thoughts racing even more, it helps me find a solution. It opens new doors for me.

I could tell my teacher wanted me to get this guy in trouble. He never specifically said so, but I could tell in his tone. What I took out the most out of our talk was this:

"I don't want to ruin his life."
He took a deep breath.

"Yeah, but what has he done to yours?"

It blew me away. I never even thought about it from that angle… Then he started talking to me about how I would feel if I found out that it happened to another girl. I thought about that a little; it's the reason that I went to the counselor in the first place. But hearing it from someone else too well, he changed my perspective. I still wasn't entirely convinced to turn him in, but I was thinking about it. I really didn't want to ruin his life. You see, he really doesn't know what he wants to do. One day it's to go into the National Guard, the next it's to be an auto mechanic. I didn't want to mess up his plans even more. I want him to be successful and happy, even if he ruined so much for me. He ruined my trust foundation for not just my future boyfriend, but every other relationship in my life; even with my mom, or teachers. Or friendship. I lost trust for almost everyone.

I needed to get it out more. There wasn't anyone that I seemed to be able to tell the whole story to. I could trust Emily, but there were always people around us so I couldn't say much because people eavesdrop. I'm pretty sure her friend Juliana heard our entire conversation during choir, but I believe that I can trust her too. Heidi and I were getting along so I just told her I needed to tell her something, but she had to promise not to tell anyone. She told me that I could trust her, so I did. Big mistake. All I said was, "I got raped." As soon as she said, "By who?" I knew she didn't really care. All she wanted to know was by who, not if I was okay or anything. So, I didn't answer her. "By who? By who?" She kept sending it and sending it, and the next day, people somehow knew. People somehow found out, and I got teased. Remember how I talked to Emily because I trusted her? That was so wrong of me. I texted Heidi and asked why she told people, and I told her she was the only person I told. I left out Emily and my teacher. She started spazzing out saying she had several people that, "I told," tell her. What the heck? Emily must have told people. Wait... Maybe it was Juliana. I did think she was listening. I asked Heidi why she told people and she flipped out saying it doesn't matter. I was so confused. Heidi started texting me and calling me a liar and saying that none of this ever happened. Heidi started telling me that I never got raped. Heidi and Luke are always together, so of course when he found out he started trying to make my life a living hell. He started rumors about me. Very false rumors. But of course, with all the girls he has on their knees for him, they tell everyone once he says it to them. Luke's friends call me a liar as they walk past me in the halls, and I get many texts saying, "Is it true?" Or my favorite, "Why are you doing this?" Heidi and Emily hung out that day during school a lot, so I got a lot of laughs, whispers and eyerolls directed towards me. I wanted to give up. I started skipping my classes and hiding in the bathroom. I started crying and freaking out. I didn't know what to do. I was hopeless.

You see, this is why people who get raped are too scared to come forward. Everybody says, "He wouldn't do that, she wouldn't do that." People make excuses. People don't believe you. I'm 15 years old and I think about this everyday. The fear inside me hasn't gone away and it's been over a month. This weekend, I went to a waterpark with my family but I had to leave right away because I was so, so scared that it might happen again. Grown men looked at my body like it was a piece of meat, and I was scared. I was so freaking scared. And the shitty part is, I don't think this fear will ever go away. I never used to think twice about it. "It won't happen to me." But guess what, it did happen to me. It happened to me, and it could happen to you.

LIII

The Aftermath

Instead of sitting by me in personal finance, he sat by the girl that he always called a whale. He sat next to the group of girls that he always made fun of. It hurt really bad. I tried to keep my cool. *Alright, just don't look. Yeah, that will help. Talk to someone.* I faced the wall of computers but saw his reflection. *Shit.* I turned to my friend Jordan and tried to distract myself. It's been over a month since I was able to call him mine, and it still hurts. I love him so much. I constantly get sent pictures of him with other girls. He's been with so many since he had me... I wasn't enough for him. For so long, he was all that I had. He was always there, and I loved it. I loved having him there for me whenever I needed him. I loved if I was sad, he was right there to hold me, and loved spending time with him. If he isn't the one, I wonder how amazing it will feel with the right one. I wonder how bad it will hurt when the right one leaves. Wait, the right one won't leave, dumby.

I've never gone through a heartbreak as terrible as this one. The pain, it's starting to fade. I try to distract myself a lot. Just, sometimes it hits me at random times. When I can't sleep. When I wake up in the morning. When something good happens to me. It's becoming less frequent. It's becoming less severe, and I'm thankful for that. He's been with a lot of girls in the time that we've been broken up.

LIV

It's been over two months now. I
haven't even looked at a guy
romantically. I talked to a guy from my
school for a while but he just
attempted to use me. Once the word got
out that Luke and I broke up, I got
lots of texts from guys. I was pretty
much like, "Oh yeah! Let's get ourself
into the same situation! Let's get our
heart broken, yay!" I got asked on a
shit ton of dates, but I knew I wasn't
ready. Funny. He's getting laid and
partying, and well, being happy. And
I'm a wreck. I'm a mess. I'm less of a
mess than before, but I'm nowhere near
happy.

Now, he's telling everyone that I
told the cops that he raped me. I
didn't. I kept it to myself and let it

destroy me. Yet, he's telling everyone that I did. Why? Well, he wasn't accepted into the National Guard because of his academic scoring, and he needed an excuse. So, he picked me. The funny thing is, the Sergeant for our area, talked to my mom a couple days before this incident. He asked if she would tutor him, because he is lacking a lot of things that is needed. I was there. She told him that if he's interested, she will, but she doubts he will because her daughter and him just broke up. So, there we have it. I get more texts calling me horrible names. Now he's just playing victim. I did nothing wrong. I didn't turn him in just to avoid ruining his future. I didn't turn him in so that we don't hate each other. I didn't turn him in to avoid this. I wanted him to be successful, and happy. And because he's not at the moment, he's blaming me. He needed someone to blame, other than himself. Everyone is against me now. Everyone thinks that I made up a story to ruin his life, when it is in fact, the exact opposite.

LV

My biggest mistake

So, a major part of my trust issues revolve around one person named Heidi. She's been mentioned many times before. I've written about her so many times, I just got scared and deleted it. Back in fourth grade, we became best friends. She has always been a people pleaser. Even though we were, "best friends," she would tell all of my secrets to anyone who asked, just because she wanted to please whoever she was talking to at the moment. That isn't really the kind of person people should be around. I had a lot of good times with her; she was really funny and fun to be around. When you're with her, it's fun and drama free. Just talk about life and problems, but when you would leave, she would tell everyone that she talked to exactly what you said. She doesn't ever mention that she talked about you though, of course.

We were really good friends up until seventh grade. We weren't as close. Ever since then, even though we don't talk, she finds ways to make my life suck a little more. She starts almost all of the drama in my grade. There's been several situations where she just makes me feel like complete shit. She never feels bad for it either. She loves drama and I don't know why. Maybe the attention? Still, why would someone like making people feel bad? That's like the complete opposite of me, to be honest with you.

So, how does she fit into this story? Well, like I said, she always does anything she can to ruin my day or start drama. I don't even think she realizes that she does it. It's taken over her. It really bugs me because we used to be such great friends, but she's so different now. She's hilarious and nice for the most part, she just cares too much about what people think of her. It's really sad.

She always uses my past against me, which is funny considering she doesn't know basically anything about me. She tries to make me feel guilty for trying to kill myself. She likes to kind of laugh about it, which really bugs me. It's the kind of people, like her, that I wish would change. She just jumps to conclusions and says stupid things when she doesn't know anything about the situation in the first place. Like, she's the type of person who you would be having a fun time with, than all of a sudden she'd say, "Oh my gosh, I remember the time that you glared at me in sixth grade." And then get mad because of that. It really angers me. She does anything to ruin my days and I could write a lot about certain situations, but she isn't worth my time.

I just had to get this out because she really made me mad today. She was basically calling me a bad person. She knows something that could ruin a lot for me. She threatened to tell everyone, then she said every time someone talks bad about me, she is just going to laugh, agree, and participate. What a swell individual, am I right? She isn't a bad person, she just really likes drama. I don't know.

I didn't mean to put this in my book, but I had to get it out. Might as well turn it into a life lesson for you. Don't assume things. Don't make fun of people's choices or use them against them. I don't mean a major crime like murder or something, I mean like, having sex at 16, stealing $20 from their mom, sending inappropriate photographs of themselves. You have no idea why they did it. You have no idea what was going through their mind, only they do. You are not them, so leave them be. Maybe they regret their decision, maybe they would take it back if they could. They did it, and it's in the past. If they are trying to get better, don't bring it up. They're doing something positive and you just keep pushing them further and further from their goal… Leave them be.

So, when I get teased for suicide attempts, it really brings me down. I mean, these people know nothing about me and have the nerve to try and tell me that I am stupid. Heidi has done this several times too. I know that it's not something to be proud of, but I am trying so hard to get better. I am seriously trying so hard. But, then there's people who think that they're okay with teasing me about something I am trying to improve. They don't consider the factors. They just think, "stupid!" Before anything else. They just don't know. They don't think, "Wow, she must have been hurting beyond words to try to take her own life." Instead, they take it as an opportunity to make fun of me.

It's the same with cutting. I can't begin to tell you the amount of funny looks and negative remarks I have gotten. I don't want to be this way but they don't understand that. I bet that they would maybe want to more if they got a taste of it. Or at least be more understanding.

Then again, there are so many bad people in this world. There are so many people who like putting people down. It makes them feel better about themselves. I will never understand how, but it does. It empowers them to see people suffer. It's what they desire. It's sad how many people like that there are in this world. I wish there were so many less, if not none.

Guys, if you know someone like this, try so hard not to let them get to you. They want to get a reaction out of you. It's what they want. They want to make you depressed, they want you not be successful. So, guess what you need to do? Don't give them what they want. If you know you made a mistake and you want to change that and are working towards it, don't let it get to you. You know what you want. You know why you did it and you are trying to get better. I'm proud of you. It doesn't matter what anyone else thinks or says, it's about you. What you know and believe. You can get through this. You can get over the bad people. You got this.

I was so stupid for trusting her again. I don't exactly know why I did. Maybe it's the fact that I still miss our old friendship. We were best friends for so long, and I wish she hadn't changed. I wish she didn't care so much about what people thought of her, and I wish she didn't get joy out of making others feel like shit. I wish she hadn't changed, but guess what? People change. It could be bad in your eyes, and good in someone else's. Who knows? It's just part of life, and I believe that everybody goes through changes in their life. Like I mentioned before, I wrote about her so many times, but I was so scared and deleted it just about every time. Heidi, well, let's not sugar coat it. She is a bully. A giant bully. She is so mean to so many people, and I wish she wasn't. The things she says are just so cruel, and not just to me. I could fill several rooms full of people who would agree that Heidi has intentionally hurt them. She is the person that spreads

the false rumors about me. I wrote this
awhile ago on instagram:

LVI

An open letter to the girl that ruined my life.

"If you think this about you, it probably is. You're getting ready to screenshot this and send it to all of your friends, because that's what you do. You will text them, and tell them that I'm being a bully. When I in fact, am standing up for myself. I'm not saying your name. I'm not telling anyone who this is about, but most people will know. Most people know that you're the reason behind most of my tears. Most people will know that you're the reason I lost all of my friends. Most people will know you're a huge reason I skip class and dread going to school. You're the reason I can't have friendships, because you shattered the idea of any hope for future relationships with anyone. I thought everyone would continue to lie to me, and throw me under the bus, just like you did to me for so many years.

You play victim. If we fight, you try to blame the entire situation on me. You turn everyone against me. You get joy out of seeing me suffer, and I'm here to tell you...you aren't going to get what you want anymore. You aren't going to control my emotions. You aren't going to hurt me. You aren't going to walk over me. You can turn everyone against me some more if you'd like. Hard to do it anymore than you already have. Are you jealous? There really isn't anything to be jealous of. You're pretty. And, it's not like I'm popular or anything. There really isn't a reason to push me down, besides that I'm an easy target. I'm weak. I spend most of my time at school alone, but that isn't entirely your fault, I guess. I don't like drama, and if I step out of my circle, there it is. So, I stay alone usually. Sometimes I'll joke around with some of the guys, but not very often. So, go ahead. Talk about me. I mean, you can't control me anymore, but you can control the way people see me. You've been doing this to me for far too long. I've tried texting you, but there it is, my fault. It's always my fault; never yours. You hurt me. You hurt me so much and it's a vicious cycle. It isn't just me. I see you treat other people the same exact way, and I'm so sick of it. I'm done letting you hurt me"

Heidi has told people that I am not doing anything but wasting my time with my book, and that I am telling people that it's okay to kill themselves or hurt themselves. She said that I am never going to make a difference in this world. But, well, I'm here to prove her wrong. I'm almost positive that you have a Heidi in your life. You have someone that thinks they know what's best for you, and put you down for their own enjoyment. Well, guess what? You are capable of so much more than they make you feel. Honestly, if I gave into her stupid words, you'd be reading about a 15 year old committing suicide on some article shared around on Facebook, not this book. You can't let that one person belittle you. You can't let one person destroy your dreams. This is your life,

man. Do what you want. Be who you want
to be, and don't let anyone stop you.

LV11

Suicide

I spent the weekend at my dad's house, and the break up with my parents is still is as difficult as it was the last time that I was there. I'm just glad I'm not so much into the constant fighting as I was this summer. I miss that house so much. There are so many memories attached to it. Good and bad, of course. I miss the beautiful sun waking me up in the morning. I miss the birds at the feeders. I miss my old forts, I miss the dogs running in to wake us up. I miss having a family. I miss it so much, but I can't admit it to anyone. I will admit it to you, though. I was having a very rough time.

For the second time since my last suicide attempt, I spent the night there. The time before, I was super sick so I just slept the whole time. I was taking it hard the whole weekend. The drawings in the closet are from the beginning of seventh grade. The crowns on my shelves are from my pageant days. The stain on my carpet was from when I took my mom's makeup and dropped it and it broke all over. I found one of my old baby teeth in a giant pink plastic tooth and all that I could do was laugh. I found old notes and drawings from Elementary School.

It was hitting me hard again. My dad was talking about how important grades are. I have mostly A's, but two F's. I really want to try but I just can't push myself enough. I'm going to start trying my best even though I hate school with a burning passion. My dad was also super angry about me getting another dog.

After a weekend of reminiscing, I headed to my mom's house. My friend, Christopher, came over for a couple of minutes just to talk. You know that I can't cry in front of people, so basically, I was on the edge the entire time. I scrunched my eyes together and held my breath. I cannot seem weak. For me, when I see other people cry I am so impressed that they are so strong, but when I do it, I feel weak. It's weird.

He wasn't there for long, but some girl in my grade, well, Heidi - surprising right? - was spreading rumors about me saying crap that wasn't true, so that made me super aggravated. Overall, I just had so many things piling up and I just wanted it to be done.

As soon as Christopher walked up the stairs, it was like a pipe burst inside of me. I went into my room and locked my door. I put both hands up and bunched my hair together and paced, unable to breath. My eyes jumped to and from every object in the dimly lit bedroom. What do I do? I missed Luke. I didn't want to see him with another girl. I wanted real friends. I wanted to be loved and appreciated. *Spider webs, dresser, Xbox.* I was sick of everything going wrong and nothing seeming to go right. *Bed. Chair. TV.* I really need to stop this. *Pop cans. Mirror.*

The tears seemed to be having a contest to who could go the fastest, and my brain and my heart fought over what to do. My body was a battlefield and I wanted it to stop. *Kill yourself. Just do it already.* I kept getting talked into this by my own head. I kept getting talked into dying but I really didn't want to. I need to live. I have to help people. I started pacing faster and my dogs nervous eyes followed my every move.

I continued to analyze the room. I noticed just about everything, about everything. I walked around the bedroom touching many different objects. I slammed my body against the wall and screamed. The wall rumbled. As the pleas for help left my body, the sadness seemed to multiply. My thoughts were at blistering pace, and breathing was thick. I felt dead.

Then, I looked at my phone. All of a sudden, everything slowed down. My blurry eyes looked around confused. My friend Christopher texted me. He could help me. I sent him a snapchat and told him I needed his help and he really didn't try to help much. I threw my phone down and grabbed my knife. *No one cares about you.* I spent a couple minutes staring down at the sharp blade watching my reflection. *Ugly.*

I looked off wondering if I really wanted to do this. I heard my phone buzzing. I had a couple of Snapchats. I quickly checked them. Finally. Christopher maybe could help. I got ready, but I couldn't stir up the words to say. I didn't know how to say it. Christopher and I have just recently become friends. I didn't know how he'd react. I thought maybe he'd go away just like Seth and Luke. I thought I would lose another important person in my life. I couldn't afford that at all.

I thought about it for a couple of minutes. I started panicking and probably did the worst thing that I could have possibly done. I sent him a picture of my knife. Now, I would for sure lose him. I mean, who wouldn't be weirded out by that? I called myself a couple of names, but it quickly followed with a deep breath. Christopher freaked out and kept calling me. *This couldn't get any worse.* I put my phone away and continued to cry and walk around. I continued to try to grasp ahold of at least one thought, but they were all jumping around inside my head having an amazing time. I lifted my fist up to punch the wall but put it down after a few moments. I wanted to go away so bad. I wanted to leave everything behind. I thought that I was ready.

I started to talk to Christopher and then he says, "I'm sorry. I called." I was really confused. I was already seeking help from my mom, so I just asked her if Chris called her. She was four and a half hours away. She was as confused as I was. I kept asking who, but all that he would do was apologize.

I just ignored him and put on my boots to go calm down. I walked outside. It was beautiful. I walked around the five acre property for quite a bit of time. I felt so much better. I went and picked apart at old objects in the woods and dug through bins with different medals in it, I attempted to make another fort.

I was at ease. I kept telling myself, "This won't matter in ten years. Not even five." I kept trying to convince myself to stay positive and it was working. My phone kept buzzing as I watched the traffic go by and thought about how I was going to spend my day. I decided to make a new youtube video. I started walking towards the house, but my phone went off again and I checked it.

Christopher finally told me who he called. 911. Just as I looked up, a cop car pulled in. My eyes scanned the area. I was scared. I didn't know what to do. The cop car must have parked up front because I didn't see him. I shouldn't run, should I? No, then he will think I'm guilty of something.

I looked around trying to gather my thoughts. The branches beneath my feet crunched as I slowly went towards my house. When I got halfway, I called for my dogs. They didn't even notice that anyone was there. There weren't any barks. I turned the garage knob, and took a step in.

Here we go. A flashlight swept across my face and my brothers fingers pointed towards me. I walked up the steps and into the house. "Do you know why I'm here?" The officer met me at the door and yelled in my face. I nodded. I got very scared very fast.

He asked me to come outside. I went to grab my phone because it was falling out of my pocket, but he demanded that I put my hands up first. He asked if I had a knife, and I said no. He checked me and there wasn't one. He asked me a lot of questions, I told the truth and of course, I cried.

I was honest, and let me tell you something, he started off doing his job. He got all of my information, my parents information, and everything else. I thought that this was going to be the same thing. The same conversation, the same questions. The same disappointment.

Then things changed. He started asking personal questions. He really tried to help me, and not because it was his job, it was because he wanted to. He gave me advice and told me how important my life was. He asked questions about Luke, and my parents and Christopher, and not having many friends, and he really helped me a lot with that. This guy, made me feel so much better, and it was because he actually cared about me.

All that he needs to do is get my story straight, call the suicide prevention lifeline, and we all talk about what to do and how to prevent it in the future. This guy went beyond his job. He wasn't just being a cop, he was being a caring person, and it means more to me than he will ever know.

I wasn't scared anymore. He wanted to help me. It wasn't fake, or just pretend, I could tell that he really cared about me. I could tell that he cared about me as a human being. He cared about my existence. Isn't that something? This time was much different than the last time.

The last time was back in August. I was in the hospital, I got to talk to a cop and he didn't do anything extra than what he had to. Neither did anyone else. Nobody said anything supportive.

Not one single person asked how I was doing. I just took a bunch of pills. I tried to take my beautiful life away, and I got ignored. I needed someone to talk to. Laying there by myself, I really didn't want to be alive. I never got help. I never had anyone talk to me besides for information.

I felt so alone and that's the opposite feeling that someone should experience in that situation. You need to at least try to help them. Just the effort makes a major difference. So, I was very happy when this stranger put in such an effort to make sure that I was alright.

Next, we have to call the Suicide Prevention Hotline. I actually tried calling it that day just to show Chris how lame it was, and it hasn't changed. Still a robot. Still have to wait awhile to speak with a real human being. I've had to talk to them three times now, but this time was also different. When we got ahold of someone, the lady wanted to know why I was upset. She asked the dumb questions first then tried to actually help me - kind of. It wasn't like the cop, but she showed some type of attempt to help me.

Overall, I was impressed and very satisfied. I explained my story. I was able to stay positive enough to not do anything stupid. I told them, yes, I really did want to, but I am better than that now. I am getting better.

Let's face it, if this all were to happen a couple months ago, there's no doubt in my mind that I would not be able to handle everything getting thrown at me. I just know that I couldn't. I know because the want to be saved, is the highest it's ever been. The want for everything to be quiet is the highest it's ever been. The want to fall asleep forever and never wake up, is the highest it's ever been. The want to pull the trigger is the highest that it's ever been.

But you know what? The want to be successful is higher than it's ever been. The want to stay alive is higher than it's ever been. I've grown so much throughout this book. I'm better. I'm so much better guys. I've been through hell and back, but I'm getting better.

Then again, I know it'll get bad again. Then it'll get terrible. I'll want to die. I'll wonder why I am even alive, but I also know that it'll get better again. Speaking in all honesty, that's sometimes all that you have to hold onto.

I'd like to write some amazing happy ending and make everyone think that life is going to be better tomorrow, but I can't. I've waited over two years for things to get better, and they have. But they also get worse, and life will continue to throw things at me, and at you and everyone else.

Life isn't a fairy tale. This is life. Depression or not, life just sucks sometimes. Life sucks for everyone no matter who you are, but I believe -no, I know- that you are strong enough to overcome anything that gets thrown in your path.

You were put here for a beautiful reason. Trust me, if I can do it, so can you. You can and will. I believe with everything that I have that you are going to do great things in this world. I don't even know you, but I would bet money that you are beautiful and that you are strong and just, wow. Yeah, you're wow. An amazing wow.

So, I didn't say goodbye. I didn't give up because I don't want to die. The truth is, there are so many beautiful things in this world, including yourself. I'm not ready to write the ending of my story because well, my story isn't over yet;

Made in the USA
Lexington, KY
09 August 2017